W9-AEJ-525

LADY BIRD
and
HER DAUGHTERS

*

by the author of

PRINCESS MARGARET

GOLDEN BOATS FROM BURMA

THE SAWDUST TRAIL

MR. JEFFERSON'S LADIES

JACQUELINE KENNEDY
(co-author with Ann Pinchot)

LADY BIRD
and
HER DAUGHTERS

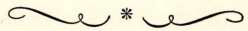

GORDON LANGLEY

HALL

Macrae Smith Company

PHILADELPHIA

WINGATE COLLEGE LIBRARY
WINGATE, N. C.

COPYRIGHT © 1967 BY GORDON LANGLEY HALL

All rights reserved. No part of this book may be reproduced in any form without permission in writing from the publisher, except by a reviewer, who may quote brief passages in a review to be printed in a magazine or newspaper.

Library of Congress Catalog Card Number 66-26497

MANUFACTURED IN THE UNITED STATES OF AMERICA

6703

For

MARGARET RUTHERFORD

and STRINGER DAVIS

Two Good Friends of America

35081

Author's Note

*

I would like to express my thanks to the Hawaii State Archives for their help in compiling the chapter dealing with Miss Lynda Bird Johnson's visit to that lovely state; the Austin (Texas) Public Library; the Smithsonian Institution, Washington, D.C.; Miss Virginia Rugheimer, Librarian, and her able staff at the Charleston Library Society, Charleston, South Carolina; Marjorie L. Morse, Public Relations Office, Georgetown University, Washington, D.C.; Mrs. William Jenkins Foster; Mrs. Roy B. (Verona Florentine) Adams of Denver; my secretary, Mrs. Joseph Allen McNerney ("Miss Gladys"); my typist, Mrs. Gertrude Young; and John-Paul Simmons.

GORDON LANGLEY HALL

The Dr. Joseph Johnson House
Charleston, South Carolina
1966

Contents

*

Perhaps you remember the most beautiful description in literature of the ideal woman. In the words of Solomon:

"She looketh well to the ways of her household, and eateth not the bread of idleness. Her husband is known in the gates, where he sitteth among the elders of the land; she stretcheth out her hand to the poor; yea, she reacheth forth her hands to the needy; her children arise up, and call her blessed; her husband also, and he praiseth her. Strength and beauty are her clothing; and she shall laugh in the latter day."

FROM *"The Total Woman,"* a baccalaureate address given by Mrs. Lyndon Baines Johnson at Radcliffe College, Cambridge, Massachusetts, June 9, 1964.

Prologue

*

WEDNESDAY, November the seventeenth, nineteen hundred and sixty-five, was her thirty-first wedding anniversary. Wed to Lyndon Baines Johnson with a Sears-Roebuck ring costing $2.98 because in the rush he had forgotten to purchase another, who would have guessed that one day Lady Bird Taylor would be Hostess of the White House?

Now, First Lady in the land, she stood waiting in her favorite Oval Room by the side of the President. This would be Washington's social event of the year, for the guest of honor was the only sister of the Queen of England, Her Royal Highness, the Princess Margaret, and her husband, Lord Snowdon.

Lady Bird always felt at ease in the Oval Room. Perhaps it was the sense of history that permeated the very walls. "It was in this room that the first occupants of the White House, President and Mrs. Adams, used to receive guests," she once told a group of visiting writers. "Dolley Madison was the first to furnish it in yellow, and that's my favorite color."

Never had the First Lady looked more radiant. She wore her hair in a gay chignon style that suited perfectly the spirit of the occasion. Her strapless silk gown was a dazzling shade of emerald. Princess Margaret had always wanted to visit America; now it was up to Mrs. Johnson to show she was really welcome.

The guests had been chosen with great care, as *The New York Times* later commented, ". . . because of the youth and sprightliness of the couple honored tonight." The great-great-great-great-granddaughter of that same King George III who had so displeased the American colonists had already charmed their descendants with her ready wit, candor, and good common sense during her whirlwind tour of their country.

Preparation of the floral arrangements were begun at seven o'clock that morning for the tables in the State Dining Room and for the classic urns throughout the Executive Mansion. Yellow roses, symbolic of the President and his Lady's beloved Texas, mingled with heather and daisies.

The President, still recuperating from his recent operation, looked remarkably fit, although Lady Bird secretly hoped that the evening would not unduly tire him. Squab had been stuffed with wild rice as the *pièce de résistance* of the banquet menu.

Now the Princess was about to arrive. The music of the Marine Band was welcoming the guests in the great entrance hall below.

The Princess smiled at Lady Bird, who returned the greeting. They were both such tiny women beside the tall President. Fashion-conscious Margaret wore shocking pink batiste with a matching jacket edged at the low neckline and sleeves with a pearl and crystal fringe. Then, after verbal greetings were exchanged, the Johnsons presented the Snowdons with an autographed family photograph and two watercolors by Washington artist Lily Spandorf, showing Bryce Park, dedicated by the Princess earlier that day, and the statue of the late Sir Winston Churchill shortly to be erected in front of the British Embassy in Washington.

There were official photographs to be taken in the rose and white Queen's Room. This was a good choice on Lady Bird's part, for it was in this room that both Margaret's mother and sister had slept on different occasions, as had the late Queen Wilhelmina of the Netherlands, her daughter Queen Juliana, and the Queen Mother Frederika of Greece. During her visit in 1951, Queen Elizabeth, who was then still a Princess, had given the eighteenth-century overmantel and mirror "as an ornament to one of your proudest national possessions" and "a mark of our friendship, so long as the White House shall stand."

It was time now to descend the Grand Staircase. The President and Princess Margaret led the way, followed by Lord Snowdon and the First Lady. This wedding anniversary would stand out above all the others. Had it been so long ago that she had stood beside Lyndon to be married in San Antonio's historic St. Mark's Episcopal Church? They had set off for Mexico in the car he was then still paying for and would later start married life in a small one-bedroom apartment that boasted a rollaway bed in their living room. . . . Now they lived in the White House. *For Lady Bird Johnson, the young woman from Karnack, Texas, surely this was the American dream come true.*

WINGATE COLLEGE LIBRARY
WINGATE, N. C.

LADY BIRD
and
HER DAUGHTERS

*

1

Teen-agers in the White House

✳ ✳

"THE future of young women looms bright. Your horizons are not finite. You were born at the right time. *It is a good time to be a woman.* It is a good time to be alive."

The words are the First Lady's, directed at young women everywhere, including her own two daughters—Lynda Bird and Luci Baines.

America's most famous mother-and-daughters team enjoys a happy relationship of mutual love and consideration. "I have always tried to tell them, in the House and in the Senate," says Lady Bird, "in each of these jobs, to try to imbue them with a great respect for the job, for working for the country, but that their Dad was still their Daddy, and that big black car is going to turn into a pumpkin just any day. This is a very temporary lease."

The President proudly maintains that he has "the best wife and the best two daughters in the whole country." His wife's recipe for their growing up was to make them feel independent and trusted. And it took all three of them to look after the President, Lady Bird once said.

"Bird trusts her children completely," says the President, "and they know it. She doesn't nag them, but when they seek her advice she sounds like a judge as she weighs all sides. Then she lets them find the answer. I know a lot about mothers. I thought I had the best one in the world, and as a one-time school teacher I've seen a lot of mothers, but I never knew one I thought was more devoted, yet more reserved and less gushy than Bird."

Commenting on this, Lynda Bird says: "We have moral togetherness. Luci and I always know that whether Mother is with us or not she is thinking of us. Mother has never told us when to be in from a party or date. She just leaves it to our own good judgment. How can you break faith with a woman who does that?"

Sensitive Luci observes: "The pressures on my mother and father are tremendous, so you don't feel you can talk to them as easily. But we need each other more than we ever did. There are only four of us in this situation and we must all help each other. I think this helps make us closer as a family in many ways. . . . My mother has always said to me, 'Luci, please don't ever feel you can't come to me,' but the thing that keeps coming into my mind is, 'Good grief, Luci, she has all kinds of problems, so don't bother her with yours.'"

Lynda Bird's quiet sense of duty and dignity thrust upon her as the elder daughter of the President has won for her a pleasing niche with the members of the White House press corps. Watching Lynda Bird and Luci, one is reminded of the comparison between the quiet, more reserved Princess Elizabeth and the effervescent though intense personality of her sister, Princess Margaret, at the same ages. Like Margaret, as a child, Luci at times resented her elder sister's age advantage. "In this family, I come just before the dogs," she used to grumble.

Lynda Bird is the introvert of the two, keeping her troubles to herself. When they first came to live in the White

House the press would take pictures of them both, then inadvertently only use those of Luci. Lynda Bird never said a word although friends think it hurt her. What sisterly competition there was has disappeared in the past year. Happily Lady Bird can say, "As they grow older, they grow closer."

Luci's honest-to-goodness pronouncements might make good news copy, yet her sister can generate her own human interest stories. There was, for instance, that day Lynda walked unheralded into the White House press rooms. While newsmen waited, hoping she might have an important announcement to make, she bypassed them for the soft-drink machine.

Some of Lady Bird's happiest times have been passed, like any other mother in the nation, sitting at the kitchen table drinking a glass of milk with her daughters or sharing their dreams in Luci's room, which she called "a gathering-place when the girls came in from school or dates." Such moments in the life of a mother, be she First Lady of the land or First Lady in her own home, are brief, for the days of carefree youth are fleeting.

Of the President's approach to his daughters growing up, one of Luci's former dates complained: "He looks at boys like he'd look at a lobbyist. He just sits there and sizes them up, and a Lyndon Johnson size-up can scare the fool out of you."

If there was any young man he thought they should know, as a political campaign researcher once found out, Lyndon was not above hinting: "My daughter Lynda's very interested in that subject you're writing on. Why don't you talk it over with her one of these days?"

American mothers who have trouble—as most mothers do at one time or another—with their daughters staying out later than usual on a date should take courage from

Lady Bird's approach to the problem. A boyfriend who kept fourteen-year-old Luci out until one o'clock in the morning was confronted by Lady Bird. Said he: "She chewed us up one side and down the other. Nobody ever made me feel so small."

As Margaret Truman once discovered, being the President's daughter is to become overnight a public figure. Even at the University of Texas, among twenty thousand other students, Lynda Bird lived a fishbowl kind of existence. Though at times she may have complained, "I never have any privacy," she took her exacting—and often rather exasperating—role in her stride.

At the university she lived as quietly as possible, sharing a room with two other girls in the Zeta Tau Alpha sorority house. Any time she left the house Lynda Bird's shadow followed. At first, when Secret Service agents accompanied her to classes, she would sigh, "Here comes the brigade." She sometimes walked but more often rode the three blocks to campus. Either way, she had an agent with her. While she was in class he sat in a vacant seat or stood outside the classroom. On dates he was there too, and newsmen often showed up as well. Of the agents' presence on such occasions, Lynda Bird said, "It's always a case of having them hear you and your date, or see you."

The University of Texas student newspaper, the *Daily Texan,* made a point to keep Lynda Bird's name out of their columns. "It seems like the only humane thing to do," said editor Kaye Northcott.

Campus peace committees mercifully ignored Lynda's presence while she had this to say about their members: "If students are really against Vietnam, they've got a perfect right to picket. It's the ones who are rebelling just to be rebelling that I mind."

Lynda can be equally outspoken when someboby says something she does not believe to be true. The clergyman who criticized her father's anti-poverty program before a group of University of Texas Protestant Episcopal students was given quite a piece of her mind. "I'm glad that you know what goes on on the White House telephone. . . ." she scolded. "The church hasn't done anything about these problems for two thousand years. I hope you'll give my father at least a few more."

Although Lynda admits that "Caesar's daughter must be above reproach," there have been times when even she has lost patience. "If I'm drinking a glass of milk at a party it gets reported as milk punch and some nice WCTU lady will write me saying 'the sins of the flesh move upon you.'

"I never know when I'm going to wind up in print. Think what that does to my dating. If Joe asks me out and I tell him I have to study, and then I go out with Bill, what happens? Joe will read in the paper the next morning that I went out. That really happened once."

Beaux of both Lynda Bird and Luci have complained that the only way they could find any privacy was simply to stay home in the White House. One young man went so far as to say: "It takes guts to date them. You become public property after your first movie and engaged on your second hamburger."

Another complained: "If they date a guy, every other guy they date knows it too. As for the boy, if he's dating anyone else, imagine what that girl thinks."

"If one of the girls dances cheek-to-cheek," Associated Press noted, "it's front-page news. If she diets, her weight is a State Department secret. If she's engaged, ninety million females and some males want to see the ring."

Even when she goes to a movie, others in the audience are apt to pay more attention to Lynda Bird and her escort than to the screen. In a restaurant they claim more notice than they want. As Lynda Bird told a friend, "I don't necessarily think I owe my life to the American people."

"I am a blue-eyed child in a brown-eyed family," said Luci, the President's younger daughter. Her father used to tease her about this, until she settled the point when she was thirteen years old with all the innocence of youth. Addressing a racially mixed group, Luci confessed: "I don't know what to say to you folks. But I often think of my mother who has dark hair and brown eyes. My daddy and sister do, too, while I have light hair, white skin, and blue eyes. But we all get along fine together. If we do, in the same family, why can't everybody, without thinking of the color of people's skin or hair or eyes, or even how they worship God?"

For several years Luci had longed to be grown up. When her sixteenth birthday came at last, the freedom it brought was brief indeed, for with John F. Kennedy's tragic death her father was plummeted right into the Presidency. "Finally I got just a taste of it," said Luci, "and then I had it all taken away from me."

The President once told a friend that Luci did not take after himself, his wife, or Lynda Bird either in looks or temperament. "She is exactly like my mother," he declared.

At seventeen the girl who called herself "a high-strung person who likes to be happy" and one who doesn't hide her emotions, having to "learn things the hard way," found herself America's newest teen-age idol. Such adulation might well have gone to the head of any other girl, but Luci's outlook was already mature. By simply acting herself, unconsciously she began to spread goodwill amongst the young people of the nation.

As an example, hundreds of teen-agers tried to clasp Luci's hand after she had christened her first ship, the U.S.S. *Louise Lykes*, at New Orleans. In Los Angeles she shook so many hands at a "Young Citizens for Johnson" dinner that she acquired a blister. When she walked among the 1,100 guests, the waitresses were delighted to find that Luci remembered them with a cheerful handshake too.

Her mother has nothing but praise for teen-agers. She knows of no special formula for raising daughters, comparing the process to putting messages into bottles, sending them out to sea, and hoping that eventually they will float back. "When they do," she says, "how pleased you are!"

Crowned Queen of the Shenandoah Apple Blossom Festival in Winchester, Virginia, with her beaming father looking on, Luci quipped, "I've never even been a duchess before." She was referring to her sister, who in 1960 had been Duchess of Texas at the Gilmer City Yam Festival.

When she caught White House staffers misspelling her name, she told them firmly, "It is *Luci*." To close friends she likes to sign letters with a little drawing of a face, each curved line of which represents a letter in her name.

The first teen-aged daughter to grace the White House since the William Howard Tafts and their seventeen-year-old daughter Helen lived there, she adapted herself very well to such a public existence.

"Luci got sick after we had first moved in," said her mother, "and she had to stay in bed. I let her have her two dogs in her bedroom and they jumped and romped so much that I felt guilty . . . until I read in a White House guidebook that Theodore Roosevelt's children had all sorts of pets. Once he brought in a calico pony to cheer up one of his sons. I haven't brought in any horses yet."

Her father, while showing off the White House, gave another delightful family anecdote concerning Luci. Said he, "While this is the treaty room, I would like you to know that this is the room where President Johnson met with his Cabinet for the first time—President Andrew Johnson. This is also where President Lyndon Johnson signed his first treaty. In order to do it I came in here the other night and looked in the door. My daughter, Luci, was sitting at the head of the table studying plane geometry. I asked her mother if she couldn't arrange to put a desk across the hall to make a study room out of it so that if we needed the Cabinet room it would be available. We picked up the plane geometry, *Macbeth,* and a few other things and hauled them across the hall."

The warm and impulsive Luci found, like Lynda Bird, that being the President's daughter had many drawbacks when it came to shopping and dating. "I even have to order a pizza pie under a false name," she once complained. On the way to classes or out for the evening with a young man, the Secret Service man always trailed along. This could be very bothersome, as Jacqueline Kennedy in her turn had discovered on her quiet walks along the Hyannis Port shore.

One of Luci's disappointments was that she could not correspond regularly with some of the interesting youngsters her own age who wrote in from all parts of the world. Diplomatically, to each she replied: "I have received so many letters from people all over the world that I wish I had more free time to make friends by mail, but school work and home work are so time-consuming that I know you will understand why I have to say 'No' to your kind invitation to be a pen pal."

Deeply loyal to her friends, especially those who have been accused of being opportunists, Luci chose to believe that they liked her for herself and not because of her father's high position. She told this favorite story concerning her father and one of her friends:

"Of all the things I can remember my father doing, the thing that meant the most to me was the time one of my friends had a big problem and Daddy helped him. We were flying to Texas and my father sat down and talked to him and was his confidant. It was an example of Daddy going out of his way to be a friend to a friend of mine. There is nothing I want in the world than to feel the people I love, love other people I love."

Animals likewise have always occupied a special place in Luci's heart. She used to exercise the family beagles and upon first coming to the White House declared that a "high strung" white collie, presented to President Johnson by an Illinois schoolgirl, preferred her company to that of the rest of the First Family because "I'm the only one Blanco isn't afraid of."

In La Grange, Illinois, she reviewed a parade of children leading their dogs and carrying their cats in the annual pet parade. "The pets," she commented ecstatically, "were just darling."

In her early White House days, while still a student at Washington's National Cathedral School, Luci could be seen, accompanied by her Secret Service agent, rushing to make an eight-thirty morning class, attired in, among other things, white bobby socks and headscarf. Her five-dollar weekly allowance had to go a long way, having to account for extra school supplies, long-distance telephone calls, and Saturday lunches.

By the time her father had occupied the White House for a year, her warmheartedness had become legendary. When a friend of hers, a young man, was confined to a hospital for several weeks, Luci prepared lunch and dinner for him every day and took it to his bedside. The priest who tutored her in the Roman Catholic faith said: "She was very sincere. She'll be a saint."

2

The Road to Hawaii

✳ ✳

"I'm leaving my teens at last, and that's to be celebrated," was Lynda Bird's comment upon reaching her twentieth birthday on March 19, 1964.

The family observed this special landmark with a quiet dinner party, while the following week Lynda Bird left for a short visit to New York City, accompanied by Warrie Lynn Smith, who was her sorority sister at the University of Texas.

Warrie was, for a time, living at the White House while attending George Washington University. The brown-eyed girl had not been unduly fazed by the prospect of staying in so august a home. "It's very thought-provoking," she commented. "I'll be studying American history and I think the atmosphere will be very conducive to my studies."

Registering at the Hotel Carlyle, the two girls spent a crowded schedule shopping and attending the theater. While the White House was putting out feelers to find just what Lynda Bird would be wearing for the annual Easter Egg Roll which she would hostess with her sister Luci on Easter Monday, the girls saw the President's favorite musical, *Hello Dolly* starring Carol Channing, and the plays *Barefoot in the Park* and *110 in the Shade*.

By the time they arrived home at the White House, Lady Bird had already been photographed against a bank of Madonna lilies, showing her Easter finery: a three-piece coral wool suit, the short-sleeved jacket flecked with white. Her coral silk blouse had a round collar set off by a small bow at the neck. She flew down to the LBJ ranch with her husband for a restful weekend, her daughters remaining behind. By this time it was announced that Lynda Bird would wear a white linen spring suit and Luci a white woolen one.

Nobody seems to know how or why the traditional Egg Roll on the White House lawns began. Every Easter thousands of Washington children, carrying baskets of Easter eggs and accompanied by their parents, invade the grounds, where they have the run of the place for two hours. Afterward the lawn is left rather sticky from mashed jelly beans, so that it takes a platoon of gardeners to clean it up.

Both of the President's daughters have a way with children so that Lady Bird could feel free to leave the Egg Roll in their capable hands. (However, that year the Egg Roll was cancelled due to a snowstorm.) On the ranch, the President and his wife were able to relax in the enjoyment of their beloved undulating hill country of south-central Texas. The live oaks were newly in leaf. It was a time of refreshment for both the President and his lady; the pure spring air was invigorating and Lady Bird was in good form to receive an honorary doctorate of laws degree from the Texas Women's University at Denton.

Returning to the White House, they found the nation's press commenting upon Lynda Bird's early interest in politics. Gerry Van Der Heuvel, writing in the New York *News*, had this to say:

"It's enough to give the Republicans the weeping willies. They not only have to contend with the most cyclonic President in history, but the most active First Lady since Mrs. Roosevelt.

"Now, they've also got to face young Lynda Bird, who may have broken her engagement to her young Navy lieutenant but is obviously still very much with politics. During her father's poverty tour this week, she showed that she'll be a wow in the election campaign this fall.

"Lynda Bird is just 20 and a sophomore in college here. She is tall, rather pretty, and like other girls her age, interested in dances and dates and parties. But she also has a rather remarkable interest in national affairs."

The columnist further noted that Lynda Bird was "a rather pleasing combination of her father and her mother," that she had "her mother's soft Southern charm and accent, her gracious ways with people . . . her father's evangelical spirit and political instincts."

Said historian Eric Goldman, then a White House consultant: "Lynda's a real history buff. She really lights up when she gets on the subject." At the University of Texas in 1966, Lynda made honor societies in history, classics, and government. She has always been an A student.

Her father declares, "Lynda Bird can always make a living for herself." Her mother says: "Lynda Bird ought to have been a lawyer. She can talk you into anything or out of anything."

Making an unprecedented father-daughter trip in connection with the Johnson Administration's anti-poverty campaign, she delighted her audiences in six states with her short, fervent speeches made without notes. She seemed to have little fear of the platform and could hold the attention of her audience, especially the young people, to whom at one point she declared:

"We are the group that is making the Peace Corps work and we want to make the job corps work too. Someone asked me "What can I do? I am just one person in millions." . . . Maybe in the evenings you could teach somebody to write who doesn't know how. It doesn't take a college degree to be able to teach someone to be able to read and write.

"The young people, my generation, we are going to be the ones who are leading the country in another thirty years. I want to ask you also for your heart and your hand to help all of us in our war against poverty."

Her father was obviously filled with pride, notably at the receptive reaction of the large crowds. She garnished her talks with touches of humor and laughed when the President jokingly reminded her that she was both a school dropout that day and her mother's stand-in.

Seeing the President and Lynda Bird together for this whirlwind tour, one could not fail to note how much they resemble each other in looks. This resemblance is even more striking if one sees pictures of the tall young naval officer who one day was destined to live in the White House.

Lady Bird and Lynda Bird make a pleasant mother-daughter team. They harmonize beautifully, whether the occasion be a public or a private one.

In late January of 1964 when the Senate Youth Program was holding a week-long conference in Washington, it seemed most appropriate for the 102 young people taking part to visit with the First Lady and her elder daughter at the White House.

It was a jolly, informal occasion with Lady Bird serving light refreshments in the State Dining Room. Lynda Bird beamed when Lee Davis of Auburn, Alabama, pinned a large orchid corsage upon the diminutive First Lady. There were delegates from each of the fifty states and the District of Columbia.

Greeting them, Mrs. Johnson said: "I can't tell you how

happy I was to meet each of you. I just think it was marvelous that so many of you were able to come here. I've been around government for twenty-seven or twenty-eight years, and I do hope you found everything to your taste."

She was referring to the students' purpose for coming to Washington, to observe the course of government at work. Financed through a $70,000 grant from the William Randolph Hearst Foundation, the program had been specially created by a Senate resolution.

"I certainly congratulate the Hearst Foundation for sponsoring the program that made it possible for you to come," declared Mrs. Johnson, while Lynda Bird, wearing, like her mother, a vivid red dress offset with a string of pearls, discussed her own studies with the youngsters.

"Do look around while you are here," enjoined Lady Bird, so the students were taken on a tour of the White House. Earlier, at Arlington National Cemetery, Massachusetts students had placed a wreath upon the grave of the late President John F. Kennedy. The inscription upon the ribbon read: "From the Youth of America and the Senate Youth Program."

Toward the end of April 1964, the White House confirmed the news that the engagement between Lynda Bird and Lieutenant Bernard Rosenbach had been ended by "mutual agreement." Lynda Bird returned the diamond ring to the twenty-three-year-old Annapolis graduate from Comfort, Texas. According to a friend, she broke the engagement "because she knew she no longer loved him."

When questioned by reporters as to whether a difference in religion was a cause (Lynda Bird is Protestant Episcopalian and Rosenbach a Roman Catholic), Mrs. Johnson's press secretary, Mrs. Elizabeth Carpenter, adamantly replied, "No."

Rosenbach, as the prospective son-in-law of the new

President, had with the sudden death of John F. Kennedy been thrust into the public eye. Since then he had steadfastly refused to comment upon the First Family. Lynda Bird and he had undergone prolonged periods of separation caused by his tours of sea duty. At the time of the broken engagement he was stationed aboard the destroyer *Jonas B. Ingram* at Jacksonville, Florida. He declined to give a reason for the break. Lynda Bird appeared at her father's press conference, where the President announced that she was available for questioning. The reporters respected her feelings and declined to question her.

"Can you still see me?" asked a smiling Lynda Bird upon her arrival in Hawaii. Governor John A. Burns had been the first to place a lei of white carnations around her neck. Moments later she was buried up to her nose in blossoms and still the leis kept coming.

In her first official solo speechmaking appearance, which observers predicted might indicate a stepped-up role in important functions for the President's elder daughter, Lynda Bird Johnson exhibited the same warmth and personality for which her parents are known.

She arrived June 12, 1964, by Pan American World Airways at that same Honolulu International Airport where only a short year before President Kennedy had been welcomed by similar cheering crowds. Tall and slender in her green traveling outfit, Lynda Bird deviated from her pathway to shake hands with the throngs who lined the fences, giving them a spirited "Hi" or simply saying "Thank you." Most of the airport greeters were young folk waving LBJ pennants or campaign signs.

In addition to the Governor, Lieutenant-Governor William S. Richardson, and other official dignitaries, there were special representatives from among the students, such as Tom Kincaid, president of the Leilehua High School

*President and Mrs. Johnson (November 17, 1965) with Princess Margaret
and Lord Snowden in The Oval Room.*

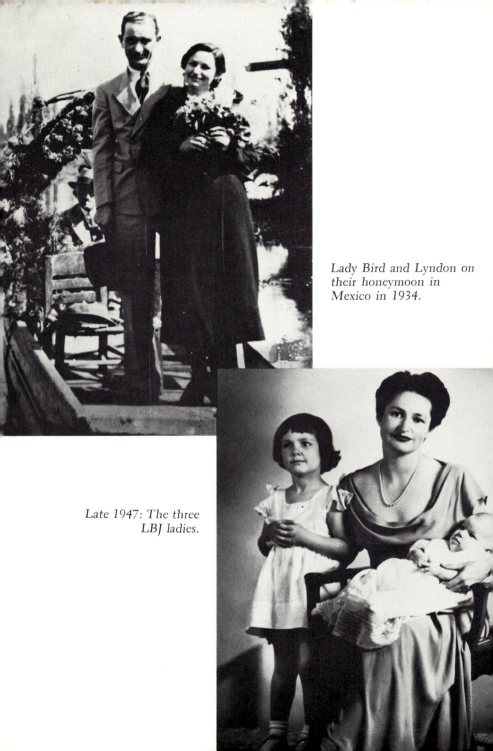

Lady Bird and Lyndon on their honeymoon in Mexico in 1934.

Late 1947: The three LBJ ladies.

Luci and Lynda with their grandmother, President Johnson's mother, and three cousins at Christmas.

Fall 1950: Lynda is 6, Luci is 3.

Lynda at age 4.

Luci at age 7.

The young fry—Lynda Bird, Beagle, and Luci Baines on the front lawn
at the ranch in 1954.

The Johnson family at Disneyland, fall 1955.

Campaigning in 1960 for the Kennedy-Johnson ticket on the
Lady Bird Special.

Luci and Lynda at the Inaugural Ball, January 1965.

Lynda Bird receiving an affectionate welcome during her first Hawaiian
vacation in June 1964.

Luci working at her summer job for a Washington
optometrist, July 1964.

An exciting day for Luci, shared with the entire family,
when she was crowned the 1965 Azalea Queen.

Lady Bird planting pansies on the Mall in Washington
is supervised by Secretary of the Interior, Stewart Udall.

Enjoying the natural beauties of our land, Lady Bird
(in front with the sunglasses and Texas hat)
is followed by rafts filled with reporters down the Colorado River.

Mrs. Johnson addresses the American Road Builders
Association, February 1966.

Lynda Bird and Mrs. Johnson greet Mr. & Mrs. Carl Sandburg and
Mr. & Mrs. Edward Steichen, spring 1964.

Mrs. Johnson and Linda posed for a formal portrait in The Yellow Oval Room on the second floor of The White House in December 1964.

Luci Johnson's formal engagement portrait, taken in the Green Room of The White House, January 1966.

Luci Johnson and Patrick Nugent at one of their engagement parties.

The entire wedding party of 26 lines up with the bride and groom on The White House steps.

Luci and Pat, with their parents, on The White House balcony.

The newlyweds, Mrs. & Mrs. Patrick John Nugent.

A fond farewell as the newlyweds leave to go on their honeymoon.

Assembly, who stood next to the Governor with a mauna loa orchid lei.

Lynda Bird was exuberant that sunny afternoon.

Considering that Lynda Bird had not been trained as an unofficial ambassadress of goodwill, she acted like a veteran at the job. "Lynda's father would have been proud of her," an observer was prompted to say. It was a brief yet warm and moving welcome, for the people of Hawaii seemed just as pleased to have her as a guest as she was to be one. One little gesture, reminiscent of her father, was made when she backtracked several steps to thank the hula troupe for their music and dancing.

Fifteen minutes later the President's elder daughter was on her way to the Hilton Hawaiian Village in the Governor's limousine.

Next day the morning began at eight with a breakfast of milk, sausages, and doughnuts served in her twelfth-floor room. Her hair was still wet from a swim at the beach when she emerged from the hotel elevator wearing a simple blue dress, high-heeled shoes, and sunglasses. Lynda Bird had already captivated those in the hotel concerned with her comfort.

"She's a very nice girl," said a hotel spokesman. "Taller than I thought, but has a beautiful smile. She's charming." Mentioning her hotel shopping activities the night before, the spokesman continued: "She didn't look at muumuus or anything like that. She was interested in bathing suits, but she didn't have much time to buy anything. She enjoyed her special catamaran cruise and says she wants to go again." (A catamaran is a boat with two hulls built side by side.)

Arriving on the university campus that morning, she joined Teuila Kaipo, secretary of Leilehua High School Assembly, the organization that had invited her to Honolulu to address the Little White House Conference on Children and Youth at Spalding Auditorium at the University of

Hawaii. Teuila has an interesting background, her racial extraction being Hawaiian, Samoan, Tongan, English, Irish, Dutch, Scottish, and Indian. She was invited to accompany the President's daughter during her stay on the campus.

The two girls attended special discussion-group meetings dealing with teen-age crime, civil rights, teen-age employment, and school dropouts. One of these concerned suspending a teen-ager from school for smoking. The group decided that teen-agers often smoke as a means to gain recognition. Lynda Bird made the suggestion that to suspend a boy or girl from school for such an act would just be "furthering the recognition" they are seeking.

She made a good impression on other girls at the conference, receiving more floral leis following the panel discussion. Teuila was curious to know the significance of the words "Daisies Don't Tell" upon the daisy handbag that she carried. Lynda Bird explained that one could not find whether "he loves me or he loves me not" merely by plucking the petals from a daisy.

"She's adorable and very friendly," was Teuila's opinion of Lynda Bird. "She asked all about us. . . . She's got a wonderful sense of humor."

Teuila said that Lynda Bird joked about being nervous at having to make her "first whole speech" later that afternoon. "When I hold up my right hand, that means applaud," she quipped, "and be sure and cry at the right time."

After a "help yourself" lunch at the East-West Center Cafeteria, Lynda Bird was introduced to eighteen girl students, each wearing a dress representative of her own nation. Later, in a women's dormitory at the center, she was given a beautiful green and violet-red sari. While three girls helped her robe, Lynda Bird, who had been plagued with photographers, ordered: "Y'all wait till I have it on. It's like taking pictures of me in the bathtub."

That afternoon in the Andrews Outdoor Theater at the University of Hawaii, she told her teen-age audience "to show what we can do to participate in the important work of the world," calling upon them to join such projects as the Peace Corps and the anti-poverty program. She advised them to educate themselves in politics and world affairs, characterizing her own generation with the catchword theme, "new idealism." Lynda Bird declared that "even the smallest contribution makes a difference and lots of small contributions make progress possible.

"The new idealism," she said, "is the belief that high aspirations and strong ideals are not inconsistent with the most practical and efficient of programs." The President's daughter noted that "we belong to the youngest generation in history," with over half the world's population under the age of twenty-five. She continued:

"Some people think that the growing youthfulness of our population is a dangerous thing, but it shouldn't be frightening to us. We should remember that Thomas Jefferson [who, incidentally, is her mother's favorite former President] wrote the Declaration of Independence at the age of thirty-three; Alexander Hamilton helped shape our Constitution at the age of thirty-two, and John F. Kennedy had already served fourteen years in the Congress when he became President at the age of forty-two. In time of war, young people are the first called to serve their country.

"Too often in time of peace we have assumed that the important work could only be trusted to older hands. Now we have the responsibility and the chance to show what we can do to participate in the important work of the world. As we assume our responsibilities, we must not lower our horizons or lose our idealism."

Lynda Bird cited the ideals of twelve-year-old Anne Frank, set down in her famous diary as she faced death in a Nazi concentration camp, and concluded:

"If we are willing to sacrifice and labor for ideals, then

we can build a world in which Anne Frank's kind of tragedy will never again darken the pages of history. We should
seek out every chance to learn more about other parts of
the world and make a special personal effort to increase
international understanding in the United States. . . . You
here in Hawaii are particularly fortunate with people coming through from so many different countries and so many
nationalities represented here."

Lynda Bird made what was her first major solo address
with ease. If she was nervous, she did not show it. Her
Southern accent was hardly noticed; the speech well delivered and delightfully received. Afterward she was given a
standing ovation. In her floral-pattern holomuu of turquoise, aqua, lavender, green, and white, Lynda Bird
seemed to be the representative of youth everywhere.

There was some disappointment over the photographs
taken on Lynda Bird's first catamaran trip, for they did not
turn out well. The hotel spokesman seemed more upset
than his distinguished visitor. Said he: "They were very
unflattering. She is a much more attractive girl than the
photos showed." Nevertheless Lynda Bird took them home
for her scrapbook.

Other highlights of her visit to the islands included a
lesson in skin diving upon Maui, where she arrived early in
the afternoon of June 15. Enjoying for the first time one of
the favorite sports of Princess Margaret and Lord Snowdon, Lynda Bird had eight skin-diving companions, including Taylor A. Pryor, owner of Sea Life Park; Mr. and Mrs.
George Bogar, and the always-present security men.

Wearing a black one-piece swimsuit, the President's
daughter "did just great," according to Pryor, in her first
quick lesson with snorkel and mask. Complete with the
necessary flippers she set out with her fellow skin divers,
while one security man watched over them from a kayak.
"She was alert to everything and asked about two dozen

very good questions out there," said Pryor when they returned after more than an hour of skin diving around Kaanapali Cliff. Their "finds" included sea urchins, pieces of coral, and a cowrie (a yellow shell used as money in some parts of Africa and Asia), which Pryor had cleaned for Lynda Bird. She was reluctant to leave the ocean, swimming with hotel guests until late afternoon.

That evening Lynda Bird was present at a large Hawaiian luau held on the beach at Lahaina which had been among her "requested activities" listed by the White House. Mr. and Mrs. Keith Tester were the hosts to the four hundred guests attending the affair given at their oceanfront home in Lynda Bird's honor.

Seated at the center of the orchid-festooned head table, and attired in a long muumuu, Lynda Bird enjoyed the legendary poi and pig helped down with contemporary strawberry soda pop. She was the recipient of several gifts, including a sectional monkeypod tray, a set of black coral jewelry, and a peacock feather lei, which visibly delighted her, for she exclaimed with pleasure, "We have peacocks on our ranch in Texas."

Again the emphasis was upon youth, students from all of Maui's high schools sharing the head table with her.

On Big Island, Lynda Bird displayed a considerable knowledge of lava rock during an hour-long tour of the volcano area near Hilo. Her personal guide was Fred T. Johnston, superintendent of Hawaii National Park, who called her "very alert," asking many pertinent questions concerning the activity of famous Kilauea Crater, which they circled. For Lynda Bird, who has studied geology at the University of Texas, it was a memorable occasion.

After a night spent at Volcano House, they took the thirteen-mile Crater Rim drive and walked across the cinder-strewn trail. At Kailua-Kona Airport she drew the biggest crowd ever known to turn out for a visiting dignitary. Among her purchases were six cans of ground Kona coffee!

A deep-sea fishing expedition on the 45-foot boat *Emma K.* featured a sun-tanned Lynda Bird, who was to catch a four-pound tuna.

More than eight hundred students from Hawaii's school and college set attended a reception for Lynda Bird on June 19 at Washington Place, when hundreds of cookies and gallons of cold drinks were served.

Complimenting the islanders by wearing a colorful blue and green floral print muumuu and a fragrant pikake lei, Lynda Bird was soon at home visiting with various groups of teen-agers representing many ethnic groups. East-West Center students enlivened the festivities by wearing their native dress. Student body officers, Girls' State participants, youth leaders—all were represented that happy afternoon.

Ione Cuelho and Lovena Correa, both Miss Hawaii contestants, danced a graceful hula in her honor, while Lynda Bird herself seemed to attract more attention than eleven other holoku-clad Miss Hawaii contestants and the 1964 Miss Filipina-Hawaii contestants.

One Indonesian told the President's daughter that she was there in order to express her gratitude for being able to study at the Center.

Although Lynda Bird politely refused offers of cookies, she did accept a gold ring from Randall Young, president of the Hawaii Chinese Youth Organization.

Particularly noticeable was the behavior of the youngsters. Nobody asked for autographs. At all times there was order.

A group of boys, just out from a long day's work at a pineapple cannery, rushed home, changed clothes, then arrived just in time to bid farewell to Lynda Bird.

"She was sweet and poised," said one young girl admiringly. A Japanese girl envied Lynda Bird her height.

When she left the Governor's Mansion, the hundreds of young guests, including the guest of honor, had all experienced a most satisfying time.

Departing for home on June 20, Lynda Bird was delayed by Secret Service agents who had quickly cancelled her 11:45 P.M. takeoff the night before when it was learned that an enraged suitor had threatened to shoot his former girl friend and her husband near the waiting lobby of Gate 15, the plane's boarding point.

The three were slated as passengers on the same flight as the President's daughter.

Governor John A. Burns escorted Lynda Bird to the airport in his black limousine about 11:30 P.M. However, the car was stopped about a hundred yards short of the plane and hurried discussions were held among Secret Service men, the police, airport officials, and Governor Burns.

The car turned around at 12:05 A.M. and returned Lynda to the hotel. Meanwhile, Secret Service men boarded the plane and the 150 passengers were ordered to disembark. They were told, "There is a problem with the baggage."

It was learned later that Secret Service officials thoroughly searched the baggage of the three persons involved in the threatened shooting.

The man who made the threats was questioned by Secret Service agents, who described him as "unstable." He was not taken to police headquarters.

The threatened couple was permitted to continue to the West Coast on the flight when it left an hour after its scheduled departure.

Only Lynda Bird, the irate suitor, and one other man who decided not to go after the incident were scratched from the passenger list.

A Pan American official said the Secret Service refused

to take "the million-to-one chance that trouble would occur on the plane or that there was anything in the baggage."

Refreshed by her holiday, Lynda Bird immediately began taking an active part in the campaign to elect her father as President of the United States in his own right. July found her on the LBJ ranch with her parents, where she posed riding a horse sidesaddle beside her father. The white-faced Herefords lazily browzed in the hot sunshine beside the driveway; proud peacocks displayed their handsome plumage among the live oaks.

In such peaceful rural surroundings the President held one of his famous lawn-chair news conferences in which he vigorously condemned "organized violence by small groups" intent upon disrupting the progress of civil rights. "Savagery of this or any other kind," he said, "is completely alien to the entire moral and political tradition of the United States. The effort to force, bully, and intimidate American citizens—to prevent them from claiming their rights under the Constitution—must be stopped."

With her campaign efforts focused upon youth, Lynda Bird hit the trail with Luci on what was described as a "coast-to-coast program of barbecues."

Lynda Bird was guest of honor at a gigantic cookout held on the lawn of Gracie Mansion, the New York City home of Mayor Robert F. Wagner. His elder son, Robert Wagner, Jr., was host for the event, which was attended by some two thousand young supporters of the President who had each contributed $10 to the "Young Citizens for Johnson."

Nobody went hungry. Before the evening was over the guests had devoured 3,000 pounds of beef, chicken, and spareribs. Lynda Bird, who had only just attended a similar calorie-inducing barbecue at Water Mill, New York, declared, "I just love barbecues," when queried how she could stand the pace. Like a true Texan's daughter, she then demonstrated that not only could she serve up a steak but she knew just how to broil one.

Mayor Wagner's speech was short and to the point.

"I predict," he said, "that this is going to be the most unpleasant, the most confusing, the most divisive and hate-making campaign in history."

After that Lynda Bird served the Mayor's son with an ample helping of spareribs. Standing in a haze of smoke while trying to protect her pretty two-piece apricot dress from being splashed by the fat, Lynda Bird begged the photographers to hurry.

Meanwhile Luci was attending youth barbecues in the Midwest, while ever-active Lady Bird was also on the campaign road.

3

Shopping, Graduation, and George Hamilton

* *

ON August 4, 1965, Lynda Bird, sunburned from archeological digging out West, arrived at New York's Hotel Carlyle to shop for clothes and see some Broadway shows.

It was a hot summer afternoon, but Lady Bird managed to look cool in her Courrèges-style white linen dress banded in her favorite yellow. Lynda Bird, who needed new outfits for her return to the University of Texas in the fall, was wearing a light blue dress with an unusual cowl neck.

An hour before the Johnsons' arrival at 3:35 P.M. there was already a feeling of excitement. Just after three, a red-haired model from dress designer Geoffrey Beene and a public relations man arrived with hat boxes, swatch books, and blue wardrobe bags. These were for the First Lady, who was also clothes hunting.

Lady Bird Johnson had gone a long way since Eugenia Lasseter had advised turning herself over to a department store and letting them do the dressing. Now the entire nation was interested in what she wore.

(Unlike many husbands who are content to let their wives choose their own clothes, and often theirs as well, the President is very particular how Lady Bird and their daughters dress, with definite ideas as to which colors and styles suit them best. Says he, "I don't like muley-lookin' things.")

Promptly at 3:15, Samuel Tourjee, resident manager of the Carlyle, and manager Samuel Lewis took their stand beneath the white and gold marquee. They chatted about other White House dignitaries who had occupied the Presidential Suite.

The First Lady and her daughter arrived in a maroon Cadillac, preceded by a gray Oldsmobile escort car. They shook hands with both managers, then passed quickly into the hotel. It was left to Bess Abel, Mrs. Johnson's blonde social secretary, who looks like Dinah Shore, to explain the purpose of their trip.

"It's a double job," she said. "Lynda Bird is looking for winter cottons, while Mrs. Johnson herself will be shopping."

When the group from Beene's left the hotel they were smiling, saying they had left the First Lady several style numbers to choose from. One confided that Mrs. Johnson was "lovely."

Later during their stay, Lady Bird was given a private showing of the Marquise line by Walter Croen. These included suits, dresses, coats, and ensembles in gabardine, doeskin, cloque, tweed, and Shetland wool. She decided on daytime clothes, needing only a minimum of fittings, which were done later at the White House.

While Mrs. Johnson saw clothes by Adele Simpson, shown by the designer's daughter, Joan Simpson, Lynda Bird accompanied by a Secret Service man visited a Seventh Avenue wholesale house. She had been much interested in the photograph of a two-piece white satin suit with green bodice appearing in the July issue of *Harper's Bazaar*. The outfit, she found, sold retail at about $125. It was made by Abe Schrader of 530 Seventh Avenue, who described Lynda Bird as being a perfect size 14. He further explained that if her mother liked the suit and two other costumes Lynda Bird had chosen, they would be purchased through Neiman-Marcus in Dallas. During her visit to Schrader's she explained that her father preferred smooth fabrics, "anything that makes ladies look slim."

When shown a pleated suit she exclaimed, "Oh, no, Daddy doesn't like pleats." Then a velvet suit was turned down with the explanation, "Daddy doesn't like anything in tones of purple."

One of her choices was a beige wool crêpe two-piece smock dress with overblouse, retailing at $65. She took the sample size, a 6, back to the hotel to show her mother.

Going through the racks herself, she took a fancy to a black and white finger-tip-length double-breasted jacket.

"What do you think of this for Texas?" she inquired of the ever-present Secret Service man.

"It might be too heavy for Texas," was his answer, but as an afterthought he said, "But you sure look nice."

By coincidence another young woman had also taken a fancy to the white and green two-piece satin suit. She was Jean Inge, who as Miss Virginia entered the Miss America contest. She had met Lynda Bird at the 1964 Azalea Festival.

Luci, the third of the Johnson women, admits to liking simple clothes. Although before her marriage her parents might have advised her, Luci made her own final choice. In 1964 she said that she had never bought a dress costing more than $65, and even then only a "formal" would have cost her that much. She liked to buy clothes with Lynda Bird at the after-Christmas sales.

After enjoying a performance of *Fiddler on the Roof*,

the Johnsons, mother and elder daughter, were almost mobbed when they left the Imperial Theater on West 45th Street.

As the crowd, some two hundred strong, surged forward, the police and Secret Service men were hard put to control it. Several reporters and photographers afterward complained of being roughed up by these gentlemen. Observers blamed the lack of police barricades at the theater entrance for all the turmoil. In the future it seemed that the First Lady might well have to add the ancient art of karate to her other accomplishments.

It was certainly an experience that neither mother nor daughter would ever forget, although they both remained calm. When a woman reporter, trying to take notes, was pushed right in the pathway of Mrs. Johnson, the First Lady, seeing her embarrassment, was quick to say: "That must be awful. I'm sorry."

The next evening the First Lady performed a good deed by attending the 502nd performance of *The Subject was Roses*.

The New York *Herald Tribune* headlines read: LADY BIRD AND LYNDA CATCH THE PLAY THAT COULD NOT DIE.

Writing in the theater news section underneath, John Molleson explained that "the play that would not die had another moment of glory, and probably took another lease on life" because of the Johnson ladies' visit.

Lynda Bird's dates with George Hamilton were bound to be expanded upon, for in addition to her own position as the President's daughter, Hamilton is one of the most promising young actors in Hollywood.

Hollywood columnist Sheilah Graham quoted Hamilton as saying: "For every girl I've ever gone with, the first question I'm asked the next day is: 'Are you going to marry her?' Now everyone in New York has been asking the same question."

Said Sheilah: "George is not talking. . . . I don't have to add that the girl everyone wants George to talk about is President Johnson's elder daughter, Lynda Baines Johnson. George was her escort at the White House dinner for Princess Margaret and Lord Snowdon . . . and her heavily chaperoned companion recently in Acapulco."

On the latter occasion she was accompanied by six Secret Service men. At the Tequila A Go-Go Dance Club she wore a blond wig to make identification difficult, but with little success.

Hamilton flew 3,500 miles to New Orleans from Spain, where the twenty-six-year-old actor was making a picture, to be with Lynda Bird on New Year's Eve. She and her college friend Warrie Lynn Smith were the guests of Representative and Mrs. Hale Boggs at the Sugar Bowl football game played between the Universities of Missouri and Florida.

George and Lynda Bird returned to New Orleans again for the Mardi Gras in February. This time she left her wig behind and openly enjoyed the colorful festival which traces its roots back to the early days when France ruled Louisiana.

By Hollywood standards, George Hamilton lives like an old-time movie star in a baronial mansion called "Grayhall" in Beverly Hills. He shares its thirty-nine high-ceilinged, antique-filled rooms with his mother, four-times-wed Anne Potter Hamilton Hunt Spalding, better known as "Teeny," and his two brothers. The mansion was once owned by Douglas Fairbanks and Mary Pickford.

With his own three-room apartment upstairs, Hamilton, who makes over $100,000 a year, lives quietly, although he does enjoy giving dinner parties that are perfect down to the smallest detail. His best Hollywood friend is fellow-actor James Mitchum, son of Bob. Hamilton supports his Southern-born mother, whom he once described as being "an Auntie Mame, but more warm and contemporary."

She, in turn, has said that George "always said he would go into the movies or advertising, because those were the two ways to get to the top fastest." His father had been a perfume company executive and a musician.

Known for his aloofness, the Memphis-born Hamilton has had to work for what he has achieved. As a teen-ager he was a switchboard operator, clerk, and baggage porter. Once he was employed by a florist. An elegant dresser, he spent some time as a male model. His mother's good friend, silent-screen actress Mae Murray, helped him plan to go to Hollywood. After playing the lead in a Palm Beach, Florida, high school production of *Brigadoon*, Hamilton felt drawn to the acting profession, driving to Hollywood in a '49 Ford.

The first few months were hard but he was persistent, eventually getting a role in *Crime and Punishment*. An MGM contract followed, and Hamilton played the part of Eleanor Parker and Robert Mitchum's son in *Home from the Hill*. To perpetuate "my image of the rich boy dabbling in pictures" he purchased a 1939 Rolls-Royce which, when he needed extra cash, could be rented out for $100 a day. It even had a cut-out section to accommodate top hats!

His role as the young Italian in *Light in the Piazza* brought him to the attention of Rossano Brazzi, who played his father. Brazzi, one of the great actors of the Italian motion picture industry, hopes to have the opportunity of directing Hamilton when the young man is older. Says Brazzi: "He has the kind of face that will be very interesting when he is thirty. Now it's too pretty, but he'll mature." Hamilton can speak both Italian and Spanish, the latter, of course, being one of Lady Bird Johnson's pet subjects. Other directors maintain that he has talent besides looks and approaches all his roles in a professional manner.

A Christian Scientist, his religion has provided a sense of

inner calm and serenity. His ready wit and penchant for providing the right kind of entertainment for the most discerning guest has earned him the loyalty of those fortunate enough to be called his friends.

At home in his $200,000 mansion, he likes nothing better than to read while sunning himself by the pool. Something of a sentimentalist, at the age of fourteen he wrote a poetic account of Sherman's march through Georgia:

> No beauty left in Atlanta town—
> No belles, no balls, no satin gowns,
> Just blacksmiths moulding war weapons of steel
> And a skidmark or two for a carriage wheel.

For weeks before Lynda Bird's birthday visit to Grayhall, a photograph of her father stood on a table in the foyer, inscribed *To George Hamilton, with warm regards from all of us, Lyndon B. Johnson.*

He had dated rich socialites, such as the former Charlotte Ford, but the daughter of the President of the United States was in a class by herself. His mother wondered what Lynda Bird was really like. Envious observers might call her son ambitious in his choice of friends, causing one postdebutante to insist: "George is not a gold digger. . . . He's known lots of girls who lead restrictive lives, and he has great success with them because apart from being fun, witty, bright, and interesting, he can think of absurd things to do on the spur of the moment that are exciting to rich girls with status, like me."

Perhaps that is what Lynda Bird saw in George Hamilton, too, yet they do have other characteristics in common. For instance, they are both tall: he 6 feet, she 5 feet 10. Both are dark-haired and both have been engaged before and broken it off, she to Bernard Rosenbach and he to actress Susan Kohner.

Lynda Bird spent her twenty-second birthday in 1966

with Hamilton in Hollywood. To mark the occasion he gave her a party at Grayhall, where she was serenaded by ten violinists in the grand ballroom.

About a hundred of Hollywood's best-known social and cinematic personalities attended this birthday-eve party. Presents arrived from the White House—an undisclosed sum of money from her parents and cosmetics from Luci. A pair of giant sunglasses from Lady Bird symbolized that Lynda Bird had "gone Hollywood."

Eddie Fisher was there to sing "When I go to sleep, I never count sheep, I count all the charms about Lynda," while the guest list included such celebrated show-business names as Natalie Wood, Greer Garson, Jill St. John, Bobby Darin, Elke Sommer, Edward G. Robinson, and Van Johnson. Afterward George took Lynda Bird to a Hollywood discotheque called the Daisy where she even danced the frug.

Lynda Bird blossomed out in some of her most stunning clothes to date, including a black swoop-backed cocktail gown set off with an outsized bow at the waist. On her finger was Hamilton's gold friendship ring set with a blue stone. She proved a great success with the movie set, who admired her sense of humor and ability to cope with every situation.

Hamilton escorted Lynda Bird on her first visit to a motion picture studio where, in celebrity-filled Hollywood, her arrival caused little stir. The President's daughter found it a pleasing experience to walk between rows of giant sound stages without being interrupted by the well-meaning and curious.

This was the second weekend that Lynda Bird and the young actor had been together, as the previous weekend he had been a guest at the LBJ ranch. The White House described the weekend as "private." Lynda Bird and George had spent their time horseback riding and touring the countryside.

When published reports intimated that the President and his wife were unhappy about their daughter's friendship with Hamilton, this was quickly denied by Press Secretary Elizabeth Carpenter, who said that they were "not unhappy" about it at all, "because their daughter is happy." Mrs. Johnson was quoted as saying that her elder daughter "is just going through a sparkling gay time, and I couldn't be happier." She thought that the move back to Texas had been a fine thing for Lynda Bird as it provided the girl with "a more natural way of life," living in a sorority house with other young women. "It was," she said, "a declaration of freedom for Lynda Bird," who had to "tailor her life to fit in with ours" at the White House. "Luci is very much at home in the world, and Lynda even more so. They wear their bonds rather lightly."

Of Lynda Bird's friendship with Hamilton her mother said sensibly: "Lynda Bird is a grown woman and very intelligent, and it's not for me to judge her relationships. I don't judge George either. I don't know him well enough."

As with every man before him who had shown the slightest interest in either of the President's daughters, Hamilton's motives were duly analyzed in the press. As a young movie actor with a promising career he was even more subject to suspicion. To Sheilah Graham he begged: "Please, please mention that I am not going to use publicity on this in any way for my benefit. When I start to prostitute myself for my career, then I'd better quit."

With his usual friendliness and honesty Hamilton would answer embarrassing questions in this fashion: "I treat the First Family and my career so that it will not be at the expense of either one. . . . I find her [Lynda Bird] very attractive. I find in her a lot of qualities I don't even want to discuss. She is hyperintelligent."

Coming to his defense, actor Eli Wallach said, "Everyone sneers that this is an actor cashing in, but I think that girl gets a kick out of being with George—it's not the other way around."

A former girl friend was even more emphatic. Said she: "To criticize George's motives is also to criticize the girl. If he has any ulterior motives, she's stupid not to notice it. I hear she's very bright, so there must be some worthwhile exchange or she'd have his number by now."

Meanwhile, with talk of romance still in the air, one of the President's favorite relatives, his niece Rebekah Alexander, twenty-two, eloped to Las Vegas with David George Shulman, twenty-three, a University of Texas student from Kilgore, Texas. They were married March 6, 1966, in a civil ceremony. The bride, black-haired and tall like Lynda Bird, is the only child of Mr. and Mrs. Birge Alexander of Fort Worth. Mrs. Alexander is President Johnson's youngest sister. Rebekah had been dating Shulman for six months. Commenting on her marriage, Rebekah, named for her grandmother, Rebekah Baines Johnson, and known in the family as "Becky," confessed: "We told Daddy right after we got back. He made us wait a week to tell Mother." The elopement, she explained, came as a "kind of a spur-of-the-moment decision," but she had long ago decided that her wedding would be quite simple and without fanfare. The Alexanders and Johnsons are close, spending much time together in Texas, so Becky's elopement surprised the First Family, too.

Because of his association with Lynda Bird, George Hamilton's draft status soon became a matter of public interest. In Washington a Selective Service spokesman told the press that Hamilton had held a draft deferment since 1961 on the grounds that his induction would result in hardship to one or more dependents. The spokesman revealed that this was learned when national headquarters asked the Selective Service director of New York City for the status and classification record of Hamilton, following published reports that he was deferred on the grounds that he was the sole support of his mother. Hamilton is registered with Local Draft Board Number 8 in New York City and is subject to its jurisdiction, although he now resides in Hollywood.

Colonel Paul V. Akst, New York City Selective Service director, was quoted as saying that on December 13, 1961, the local board classified Hamilton 3-A, giving him a dependency deferment. The files showed that this 3-A classification had been renewed three times.

Except for his classification record and age, the contents of Hamilton's file had been kept confidential, as required by the Selective Service Act.

"It is entirely up to the local board to do what it considers appropriate after it considers the contents of his file," the spokesman continued. "This headquarters has not directed the local board to review the case, to the best of my knowledge."

When Lynda Bird arrived with her escort George Hamilton at Santa Monica Civic Auditorium to attend the Oscar presentations, she received an ovation that rivaled those of the stars themselves.

Master of Ceremonies Bob Hope noted her presence with the remark: "I'm sure she feels right at home among all these beautifully dressed people, all these diamonds and furs. It's just like going to the supermarket in Texas." Lynda Bird took the quip good-naturedly.

Later, at the Oscar Ball, she was trailed by a regiment of photographers as she danced almost cheek-to-cheek with George. "I'm the only one in the room who has gotten a tan from flashbulbs," she declared with a laugh. Obviously she was enjoying her night among the stars and so were they. She met Oscar winners Julie Christie and Lee Marvin and shared a table of four with Shirley MacLaine and her brother Warren Beatty. Miss MacLaine had recently delighted Prince Philip during his Hollywood visit with her fascinating conversation.

Columnist Florabel Muir, upon being introduced to Lynda Bird by George, told her, "That's a very nice boy you've got."

"I don't know whether I've got him," came Lynda Bird's tactful reply. In her dark red high-necked evening gown, Lynda Bird appeared glamorous as any movie queen. Hollywood makeup artist George Masters, used by Zsa Zsa Gabor and the late Marilyn Monroe, was credited with Lynda Bird's transformation. Arranging her hair in what he called "the Vassar look," Masters shaped her eyebrows with a razor blade, used dark-brown eye shadow, and applied orange-colored lipstick. Said her adoring sister, Luci, at the White House as she watched the Oscar awards over television: "She's the prettiest thing there. . . . There isn't a movie star in the place who looks as beautiful as my sister!" This was borne out by one of Lynda Bird's Secret Service escorts. He declared that he didn't recognize her.

George spent Easter 1966 at the ranch with Lynda Bird and her family, where he was treated to a typical Easter Sunday dinner of steak, ranch-grown corn, green salad, South Texas strawberries, and angel-food cake.

Lynda Bird was wearing a banana-and-cream checked dress with jacket to match; Luci, a pastel pink linen and silk ensemble; and their mother, a sand beige silk coat over a jet-black princess-line dress.

The entire Johnson family flew to Mexico City in April 1966 for President Johnson's first official visit to a foreign country as Head of State. Twenty-five thousand persons were at the airport to greet them for what was described as the most tempestuous reception in the capital's history. Because of America's intervention in the Dominican Republic, the President had previously been told the United States was unpopular with Mexicans. After the First Family's reception, he exclaimed with pleasure, "Who said we couldn't go to Latin America?"

Mexico City's high altitude had an immediate effect upon Luci, who suddenly became faint. She was taken back to the plane by a White House physician but was soon able to rejoin her parents and Lynda Bird.

President Gustavo Dias Ordaz was on hand to greet the Johnsons. Said the President of the United States: "If we are to have peace in the world, we must solve the problems that cause war. While war clouds hover over certain parts of the world, we hope that day may soon come when all the world can live together in peace as do the peoples of the United States and Mexico."

President Ordaz responded by noting that the primary reason for the First Family's visit was to dedicate a statue of Abraham Lincoln, for whom Mexicans "have a very special feeling."

But it was Lady Bird, glowing with pride at her husband and daughters, who added the human touch to the auspicious occasion. Speaking in fluent Spanish, she said that to her it was "not only an official but a sentimental journey." It was in Mexico City that Lyndon and Lady Bird had honeymooned. "I came here first as a bride and fell in love with your country."

Two million Mexicans cheered the two Presidents and their families during the 9.5-mile drive from the airport to Los Piños, the Mexican President's home in Chapultepec Park. Portraits of Lyndon and Lady Bird seemed to be everywhere . . . castanets clicked and people sang. It was a gala occasion as only the Latins can make it. "I have always known the Mexican people were generous, stimulating people, but I have never seen so much inspiration," said a delighted Lyndon. The American Secret Service men, like Luci, felt the high altitude somewhat trying. Admiral George Burkley, the White House physician, was kept busy supplying oxygen.

Lady Bird made another successful talk in Spanish, which obviously pleased the busloads of Mexicans who had arrived to see her unveil the Lincoln statue, a replica of that which stands in Chicago's Lincoln Park. The Mexico City statue stands in the newly named Parque Lincoln.

President and Mrs. Johnson chose to remain as unobtrusive spectators when Lynda Bird graduated on June 4, 1966, from the University of Texas. As the same university is Lady Bird's alma mater, it was a nostalgic occasion for the First Lady.

Lynda Bird did her best to avoid unnecessary publicity at the graduation, seeking anonymity amid the other 2,400 graduates in caps and gowns. She did not attend an afternoon convocation of the 926-member senior class of her College of Arts and Sciences, from which she was graduating *cum laude* with a bachelor's degree in history.

Lynda Bird's parents made sure that they were not seated with dignitaries and other officials but with other parents. They took no part in the program. From the White House had come a request that reporters and cameramen make themselves as inconspicuous as possible.

A fanfare of six trumpets atop the 27-story tower of the main building heralded the academic procession that evening. As the graduates said goodbye to the campus, the 100-member Texas Longhorn Band played "The Eyes of Texas."

Since graduates were introduced en masse at the commencement, Lynda Bird did not have to appear separately as she would have at the college convocation, where each graduate crossed a fern-decked stage to get a certificate of graduation. The diplomas themselves would be sent out sixty to ninety days later.

Presidential Press Secretary Bill D. Moyers explained that Lynda Bird felt it would be better for the university, her fellow students, and their parents if she just attended the evening ceremonies instead of being highlighted at two events.

Lynda Bird listened intently as Francis Keppel, who recently had resigned as Assistant Secretary for Education in the Department of Health, Education, and Welfare, said in his address: "You are entering a period in which I hope it will be perfectly normal for every man and woman to serve some branch of government at some time in his working life. . . . By serving a government I mean everything— anything from membership on a school board to a term in the state legislature, from answering a call from Washington to entering high public office. All of these are vital parts of our lives; all of them urgently need the services of the best-equipped members of our society, which would certainly include our college graduates."

Of at last obtaining her graduation goal, Lynda Bird likened it to "pushing a rock uphill for years."

"It's the end of security," agreed her mother, sharing her daughter's evaluation. As Lady Bird explained, up until that time her daughter's life "has been laid out, charted." After such a heavy dose of intellectual pursuits, "It's going to be a relief for her to be in the green pastures of pleasure," said her mother. "However, I think she looks on getting out of college with mixed feelings."

On Friday, June 17, Hamilton and Lynda Bird were together again, this time in Los Angeles, where they attended a benefit dinner and ball. Hamilton was wearing a beard grown for his new movie, *The Long Ride Home*. Early next morning the couple flew to the Red Rock Canyon country of southern Utah where Hamilton was to film on location, in Zion National Park.

It was a bright sunny day as they drove along winding roads to the outdoor set. Orange- and red-colored cliffs, some a thousand feet high, formed a dramatic background.

Upon leaving Hamilton's silver Rolls-Royce, Lynda Bird rested before getting makeup applied by a Hollywood expert. Then she lunched with Hamilton, actor Glenn Ford and Mrs. Ford, and Max Baer and Harry Joe Brown, coproducers of the movie.

They ate at a wooden table set under the trees close to a large white rock known as The Great White Throne. In spite of Lynda Bird's Secret Service men, the actors and technicians took little notice of her presence. Later, wearing sunglasses and drinking from a paper cup, she watched Hamilton as he was filmed wearing a Civil War uniform.

That evening they returned to Kanab, a community of some thirteen hundred residents, where Hamilton stayed at a motel and Lynda Bird at the home of another motel operator, Whitney Parry and Mrs. Parry. They attended a rodeo to commemorate the windup of Kanab's annual Wild West Days.

On Sunday the pair rode horseback through the red, sandy hills. A few hours later Lynda Bird said goodbye to the actor and flew to Spain, the trip being a graduation present from her parents. Lynda Bird, who told Spanish newsmen upon arrival that her desire was "to get to know your country," soon found that they were more interested in whether she would marry George Hamilton. "I still have no thoughts of getting married," was her quick reply.

Hoping to see the country as a tourist and not as a visiting celebrity, Lynda Bird had more than her fair share of trouble with eager-beaver photographers. More than once she begged, "*Nada mas.* . . . No more." She refused an offer from the Spanish Air Force to put a DC-3 at her disposal, explaining that she preferred to travel by unmarked train, auto, or commercial plane. She diplomatically declined an invitation to a bullfight with the comment, "I've seen enough bulls down at the ranch to satisfy me."

In the company of her hostess, Mrs. Angier Biddle Duke, wife of the United States Ambassador to Spain, and a former college classmate, Susan Schein of New York, she visited the palace of Spain's former kings in Madrid, where the photographers downed their cameras in anger upon being told that they could not accompany her inside.

At Toledo Cathedral, where she was particularly interested in its links with the artist El Greco, she told a photographer who persisted in snapping her: "I note there's a sign prohibiting photographs from being taken. If I obey the rule, why don't the photographers?"

At Philip II's famed Escorial she inquired if it wasn't correct that he had four wives. It was, including Bloody Mary of England. "Why wasn't Philip V buried there?" He wasn't because he hated its royal vault, being entombed instead at La Granja. "Why was Isabel II buried in the row containing the bodies of the kings?" It was explained that this was because Isabel, like the present Elizabeth II of England, was a sovereign in her own right.

She toured the grim Valley of the Fallen—a Spanish Civil War memorial carved from a sheer mountainside close to Madrid—unveiled a bust of her father which was a copy of a bronze executed by New York sculptor Leo Cherne, in the patio of the American Embassy in Madrid, and explored the fabled city of Seville in Andalusia. Alhambra, the hilltop Moorish fortress and palace, one of the finest examples of Arabic architecture in the world, was high on her list of praise. For a few seconds she stood in contemplation by the tombs of King Ferdinand and Queen Isabella, who were instrumental in helping Columbus make his historic voyage of discovery to the New World. The Spanish followed her visit with pleasure, while bachelors called her far prettier than her photographs. Among the eligible young men invited to meet her was handsome David Niven, Jr., twenty-nine, son of the actor.

On the island of Majorca, Lynda Bird represented U.S. Secretary of State Dean Rusk at a swearing-in ceremony held in the port city of Palma de Mallorca. Upon departing, her commercial plane was delayed by an unidentified Spanish woman "in yellow" who declared, "I'm not flying on this plane." The Secret Service agents took Lynda Bird off the plane while all the baggage was searched. Lynda Bird was much amused by the incident, remarking, "This is the biggest thing that has happened since the flat tire." She was referring to a flat tire that earlier in the trip had "grounded" the ever-present Secret Service escorts who were following her.

4

The Conversion of Luci

* *

"I AM happiest when I am in church," declared Luci Johnson, described by her father as "deeply religious." In January 1965 it was announced that Luci Baines Johnson was taking instruction in the Roman Catholic faith.

At that time a White House spokesman said that the family considered it a "personal and private matter. They want Luci to be able to decide freely on her own."

President and Mrs. Johnson were reported to be taking a tolerant attitude toward the possibility of Luci introducing another religious denomination into the First Family. He is a member of the Disciples of Christ Church, while she and their elder daughter are Episcopalians. At the time Luci was also an Episcopalian.

Changing her faith was no sudden thing for the President's younger daughter, who, from the age of ten, had often discussed the Roman Catholic religion with her dear friend Beth Jenkins. Beth, a Roman Catholic, recalls that when Luci was a weekend guest with the Jenkins family she would accompany them to Mass. Unlike many non-Catholics who sat through the service, Luci, Beth noticed, stood and knelt when they did. As the years passed the two girls often talked of Beth's faith, particularly regarding devotion to the Virgin Mary and the important subject of confession that at first troubled Luci. Beth's crucifix, rosary, and missal fascinated her friend.

When Luci was twelve she made up her mind to change her religion, asking her parents about the possibility of taking instruction. The Johnsons acted sensibly, advising her that she was much too young to take such an important step. Later, if she had not changed her mind, she would be of an age to decide for herself. Today they approve of her conversion.

"She's been heading toward this for a long time," was Elizabeth Carpenter's comment. "She's been heading toward it all her life."

Although Luci has often said of herself, "I am a theatrical person," there was no trace of the dramatic in what she did. She had meditated long before making so drastic a decision. Even Katharine Lee, the headmistress of the National Cathedral School for Girls in Washington, a Protestant Episcopal institution, said in an interview that Luci, "the tender plant" in whom there was "a great sweetness," had now found "spiritual strength and expression." Miss Lee spoke of Luci's "deep and real" relationship to God and her fellow man.

Luci's "searching" as she called it was no undercover thing. She spoke of it openly with both Miss Lee and the school chaplain. With Warrie Lynn Smith, Lynda Bird's friend who stayed with them for a time at the White House, she had long talks about the Catholic faith, including its changing role in the modern world, especially the current ecumenical movement. In September 1964 the President's second daughter was quietly attending an early Mass seven days a week.

"I was waiting until I was eighteen so that I could make the decision as an adult, not as a child," explained Luci, after a course of instruction that had lasted less than one year. "I found my answer in the Church. I have never been happier in my life." She had studied such books as *Constitution on the Liturgy*, which the second Vatican council had adopted in 1963; *Constitution on the Church*, approved only in 1964; and the popular *Life in Christ* by the Reverends Gerard Weber and James Killgallen. In her senior-class yearbook, Luci named the Catholic philosopher Thomas Aquinas as her inspiration.

So on July 2, 1965, on her eighteenth birthday, wearing a white lace veil, Luci entered the Roman Catholic Church. Smiling and looking serenely happy, she was baptized in the presence of her parents by Father James Montgomery at St. Matthew's Cathedral, Washington. For Luci Baines Johnson this was "a personal matter." She had simply come home.

In September Luci registered as a freshman at Georgetown University School of Nursing, a Catholic seat of learning, where she became the first daughter of an American President to study there.

Georgetown is the oldest Catholic university in the country, to which seven Presidents had already sent their sons to be educated, since its foundation in 1789—the same year that General George Washington was inaugurated as the country's first President. Five members of his family studied there, including his nephews Bushrod and Augustine Washington. John Quincy Adams was the first President to preside at a Georgetown commencement in 1825. President James Madison and his wife, the irrepressible Dolley, were sheltered at the college when the President's House was destroyed by the British in the War of 1812.

Andrew Jackson Hutchins, nephew, ward, and adopted child of President Andrew Jackson, was the first President's son to attend Georgetown. John and Smith Thompson Van

Buren, sons of President Martin Van Buren; Tazewell Tyler, son of President John Tyler; Marshall Polk, nephew and ward of President James Polk; John B. Henry, nephew of James Buchanan; and Andrew Johnson, Jr., son of President Andrew Johnson, all studied at Georgetown. Andrew Johnson's father had been succeeded by President Ulysses S. Grant by the time Andrew received his diploma—and Grant was there to hand it out. Former President Johnson and the new President were hardly on speaking terms. Johnson had not even been invited to the Grant inauguration, and the university's fine record of diplomatic relations with the White House might well have been strained if the two had met, for naturally President Johnson wished to attend his own son's graduation.

Father James Doonan, S.J., who later became the twenty-ninth President of Georgetown, left a delightful description of how a minor catastrophe was averted that day.

President Grant's secretary was Col. Robert M. Douglass, himself a recent graduate of Georgetown. The President, with his secretary, arrived at the college in the day and, of course, was assigned the first place in the front row. Everyone was in tension throughout the proceedings, momentarily expecting the entrance of ex-President Johnson.

Fortunately, however, the latter gentleman entered the college grounds only after the close of the exercises. Meanwhile, members of the faculty had been assigned the duty of entertaining President Grant.

It fell to the present writer to render the same service to ex-President Johnson, as he then was teaching the class in which his son was a member. Instructions were given that, as diplomatically as possible, the two distinguished gentlemen were not to be permitted to meet, refreshments to each being served in separate apartments of the college.

My chief concern, while entertaining ex-President Johnson, was to keep posted as to the movements of President Grant and his secretary. As soon as the two were seen driving through the college gate, Mr. Johnson was escorted, with his son Frank, to his own vehicle and, apparently well satisfied with his visit, departed. So was saved the day.

Upon entering Georgetown, Luci's dedicated goal was to become a fully fledged, registered nurse. "I'm going to give it all I can," she said, confessing, however, that she was "petrified." Luci explained that "just to be entering college is a challenge, but it will be twice as difficult to have a normal college life since I'm going with a banner across my head."

The "banner" was the White House and all that it stands for.

"I know my academic commitments will be demanding and nursing is a time-consuming field, but I am determined to devote all my time and talent to doing well."

Luci was not unfamiliar with doctors or medicine, for she had spent the summer as a very efficient assistant to Dr. Robert A. Kraskin, a Washington optometrist, doing special vision work with children. She first became interested in this field while being treated by Dr. Kraskin for an eye-focusing defect.

Honorary chairman of "Volunteers for Vision," an organization dealing with children whose sight is affected, Luci holds a similar post with "Teen Waifer," which finds homes for overseas orphans. "Luci does beautifully with kids," remarked a friend.

Of his daughter's nursing ambitions, the President, recuperating from a cold caught during his inauguration ceremonies, had this to say: "She wants to be a registered nurse. We are going to find out if she's any good and has anything on the ball."

Unlike the other student nurses in the freshman class of sixty-five, Luci did not live in; her Secret Service man accompanied her to school daily. She drove the green sports car that her father had bought for her eighteenth birthday.

Luci's four-year nursing course included such subjects as general chemistry, biology, composition and rhetoric, logic, theology, and nursing history.

School authorities said that the President's daughter would be treated like all other freshmen, with no special status or favors being shown because of her White House connections. Said a UPI correspondent:

"She'll be just another girl embarking with others on years of work and study, years of bedpans, bandages, pills, syringes, and hypodermic needles, helping what she likes to do best—heal the sick."

Luci best explained her desire to serve others when she told an interviewer: "I want love. . . . Maybe what I am trying to say is I want to love. I want to show love to everyone. So often I think of something I would like to do for someone. Thinking about it is very nice, but it is more loving if you go ahead and do it."

5

White House Bride

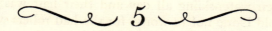

Luci's romance with twenty-two-year-old Patrick John Nugent of Waukegan, Illinois, began with a surprise meeting arranged by her best friend, Beth Jenkins.

At the time Beth was a sophomore and Patrick a senior at Marquette University. Beth recalls that Pat was like a brother to her that year. He roomed with Timothy McCormack of McHenry, Illinois, the boy she was going with.

All three were at Lake Delavan for a two-day Alpha Kappa Psi fraternity party when about midnight Beth received a call from Bill Hitchcock in Washington, a friend of hers and Luci's. It was to invite Beth to a surprise graduation party that he and Steve Steinert, with whom he used to be a page in Congress, were organizing.

Beth explained that she hadn't the fare for an airline ticket and that, in any case, she was committed to the fraternity party.

Later she told Pat Nugent and another roommate of McCormack's about the invitation. They said, "Let's go." McCormack (Mac) thought them all crazy but decided to join them anyhow. There were the three boys, Doris (Dorie)

Chistel of New Holstein, Wisconsin, and Beth. The girls had been water-skiing all day and their hair was a mess. Beth told Dorie not to worry, for she had rollers with her. As for clothes, Luci had all sizes for when she gained and lost weight.

The boys were all from northern Illinois, so they were able to stop at their homes in the middle of the night for clothes. Beth and Dorie had to make the thirteen-hour-long car ride to the White House still wearing their sports outfits.

Arriving in Washington, there was only time for the boys to get a hotel room, so the girls appeared at the Executive Mansion in sweat shirts and rumpled Bermudas.

Said Beth: "I didn't mind because I knew everyone, but Dorie was so embarrassed. The boys had planned to surprise Luci, so they kept me out of sight. First they gave her a toy nurse's kit. . . . Then they said that Georgetown University had donated a cadaver to help her practice during the summer. They put me on a stretcher and brought me in. I was giggling, but when Luci saw me she started crying.

"When the five of us got ready to leave the White House, Luci said, 'I wish I could do something wild and crazy like you all.' I said, 'Why not? Why don't you come for the prom at Marquette?' I went over to Pat and said, 'You don't have a date for the prom, do you?' He said, 'No.' I said, 'You do now.' He hadn't talked to Luci very much at the White House, but they got along great."

So Luci Johnson went to the prom in Milwaukee. Wearing a blond wig to make herself "invisible," she hid on the floorboards of cars and avoided her better-known friends. The blond wig episode didn't come to light until she was safely back in Washington, where she duly reported: "Members of the press walked up to me asking, 'Do you know where Luci Johnson is?' I didn't lie; I just evaded answering directly. I had a wonderful time," she added, her eyes sparkling mischievously. "I wanted to play, and it was a big weekend." Then, being Luci and hating to hurt anyone, she told the reporters: "I understand your problem. But I didn't want you calling and asking what size T-shirt I wear and what kind of toothpaste I use."

Two weeks after the vanishing act, Luci took over the White House. While her parents were at Camp David, Maryland, and Lynda Bird was participating in archeological exploration in Arizona, Luci gave a big dance at the White House for 250 young people, mostly sons and daughters of Washington diplomats.

She promptly ran into trouble. A Baptist minister in Florida was shocked because her young guests had been served beer. Commented Luci: "He has a right to his opinion. I have a right to mine."

Luci and Pat's friendship deepened into romance during the warm summer months after he had moved to Washington to work as an administrative assistant to the executive director of the District of Columbia Commissioners' Advisory Council on Higher Education.

He was present at Luci's baptism and attended Mass with her the next day, her confirmation and first Holy Communion. They enjoyed frequent lunches together at the White House; visited the World's Fair in New York; vacationed at the Presidential retreat, Camp David, in Maryland, and the LBJ Ranch.

Luci went to Pat's Waukegan home to attend the wedding of his older brother, Jerry, a first lieutenant in the Marine Corps who was about to leave for Vietnam.

By October rumors of a romance had infiltrated the press to such an extent that when the young couple left for the LBJ Ranch there were speculations that Pat was going to ask for Luci's hand in marriage. Upon arrival they were met by the President, who promptly inquired, "What's all this I read in the newspapers?" That, according to Luci, was "when we sat down and reasoned together."

Tall and blond, Pat Nugent is the younger son of Gerard Peter Nugent, Sr., an investment counselor, and Mrs. Nugent. Both Pat ("Nuge" to his friends) and his brother Jerry are graduates of Campion, an exclusive Jesuit boarding school in Prairie du Chien, Wisconsin. Philip Bailey, a fraternity brother from Arlington Heights, Illinois, described him as "quiet, not real outgoing, but a happy type person." Marquette professors and students called him "the typical all-American college boy." Explained one professor: "Pat is a conscientious, across-the-board student. He's independent, not one of the herd. I'd call him a take-charge guy, not a delegator of authority. When he was chairman of the interfraternity council ball, Pat did all the work himself. It was smoothly run, as though a professional cruise director had handled it. But he asked no help from his committee. He did it all himself."

The professor went on: "Pat was very popular on campus. He always dated the nicest-looking women around MU [Marquette University]."

Pat's poise, ease, and manners reflect excellent home training, according to a faculty friend. "He is not only polite but spontaneously aware of the 'niceties' such as thank-you notes when you chaperone a party or write letters of reference for him."

When Nugent left Marquette for Washington, he gave this friend a telephone number "where I can be reached any time." Knowing that Nugent was living in an apartment with a friend, the Marquette professor did not speculate about the number. When he arrived in Washington and dialed the number, a voice answered, "The White House."

Luci vows that she has never heard Pat say "a rude

thing" since the day they met. When he didn't have enough money for roses he sent her carnations. If he couldn't afford a dozen then he sent half a dozen, or even one.

After dinner he likes to lean back, smoke his pipe, and let her chatter.

After spending the Thanksgiving weekend at the Johnson ranch, Pat reported for six weeks' active duty at Lackland Air Force Base, near San Antonio, Texas. It was stated November 30 in Milwaukee that he had been a member of the Wisconsin Air National Guard for the previous three months. Lieutenant Colonel Kilian T. Morkin of the 128th Air Refueling Group, Pat's superior officer, described him as being "a quiet, serious young man who is quite willing" to perform his assigned tasks.

At last, near midnight on Christmas Eve, the long-rumored engagement was announced by President and Mrs. Johnson, shortly after the First Family and their kinsfolk gathered around the gaily decorated Christmas tree. For those close to the President's younger daughter it was not unexpected, for "whatever Luci wants, Luci gets." In a war of wills she can usually top her father when most other people cannot.

There beside the glittering tree, Pat placed a white gold engagement ring with three diamonds—a large center diamond and one smaller baguette diamond on each side—on Luci's third finger, left hand, while the President beamed his smile of approval.

The couple then attended midnight Mass at Stonewall, Texas, about two miles away. Luci, proudly displaying her ring, wore a red suit and a dark lace veil as they stood for pictures with the Reverend W. W. Schneider.

Luci's wedding was planned for the following summer. Newspapers immediately speculated where it would take place; if in the White House special permission would be needed from Roman Catholic Archbishop Patrick A. O'Boyle of Washington. A church spokesman immediately commented, "The prevailing rule is that the marriage ceremony is to take place in a church, but exceptions can be made for special reasons by authority of the local bishop." He noted that "this is an exceptional marriage." Since her baptism into the Roman Catholic faith, Luci had been a member of St. Matthew's Parish in downtown Washington.

There have been fourteen weddings actually held in the White House, the last being performed July 30, 1942, during President Franklin D. Roosevelt's third term in office, when his close aide, Harry Hopkins, married Mrs. Louise Gill Macy. The last daughter of a President to be married there was Woodrow Wilson's daughter Eleanor, who became the wife of William Gibbs McAdoo, Secretary of the Treasury, on May 7, 1914.

Before that wedding, five other daughters of Presidents were married in the White House. They were:

Maria Hester Monroe, youngest daughter of President James Monroe, to Samuel Lawrence Gouverneur, March 9, 1820.

Elizabeth Tyler, daughter of President John Tyler, to William Nevison Waller, January 31, 1842.

Nellie Grant, daughter of President Ulysses S. Grant, to Algernon Charles Sartoris of the British legation, May 21, 1874.

Alice Roosevelt, daughter of President Theodore Roosevelt, to Representative Nicholas Longworth, February 17, 1906.

Jessie Woodrow Wilson, daughter of President Woodrow Wilson, to Francis Bowes Sayre, father of the present dean of the Washington National Cathedral, November 25, 1913.

The only President to be married in the White House

was Grover Cleveland, who on June 2, 1886, was wed to Frances Folsom, twenty-seven years his junior.

Only one President's son was wed in the White House. He was John Adams, son of John Quincy Adams, who married Mary Catherine Hellen, the niece of Mrs. John Quincy Adams, on February 25, 1828.

President Wilson married Edith Bolling Galt during his first term, but the wedding took place in her Georgetown home.

Meanwhile, members of the First Family were enjoying one of their happiest Christmases. Pat telephoned his parents with the good news of the engagement. Luci also spoke to her future parents-in-law. She was delighted, commented Mrs. Nugent, who called the engagement "wonderful."

Questioned as to her son's future plans, she knew little. "Definitely he'll go on to school," she began, then confessed that this had been the plan before his engagement to the President's daughter. She said that both her sons (Jerry in the Marines was then in Okinawa) were reserved, Patrick being the more outgoing of the two. During the summers when Patrick was home from Campion Academy or Marquette University he was "too busy doing construction and other work to date."

He started in business education at Marquette, later changing to liberal arts, finally majoring in history. Noted his mother: "He wasn't quite completed with his education. He wanted to go on to school, which he still intends to do, but he wanted to get the service out of the way. He'll probably go on for a Master's degree in business."

Mrs. Nugent continued that neither she nor her husband had met or spoken to President and Mrs. Johnson, but she said with a smile, "There'll be a day when we get together."

Gerard Nugent (better known as Jerry), Patrick's father, works from an office in the simple family home located in one of the less fashionable districts of Waukegan. He is district manager for Investors Diversified Service, a distributor of mutual funds. Like Patrick, he is an unpretentious man who could well have afforded to have moved to another part of the city if his friends and customers had not lived nearby.

After the announcement of their son's engagement to the President's younger daughter, the senior Nugents received invitations from many wealthy Waukegan residents who had never noticed them before. Such overtures from fairweather friends they politely ignored. "When this wedding is all over, we'll still be living right here, doing just as we've always done," said Jerry.

Of Luci's visits he said, "She always seems to have a good time here."

"She's a good little girl," added his wife, warming to her subject. "She's always sending me notes. It's nice to know Pat and his girl really love us. In fact, both of my boys have married lovely girls."

In Patrick's boyhood neighborhood, old friends say he did not change after the engagement, insisting that he would never be "Mr. Luci Johnson." Understandably he is more retiring. After a get-together among them he was invited out for drinks but declined. Patrick's parents felt uncomfortable when Luci was visiting them and they were obliged, for her own privacy, to say that she wasn't. "But we've got to protect her," said his father. Gone were the old days when Patrick, unnoticed, could enter a beard-growing contest with the local boys. The other teen-age beards turned out to be black while his was short and red!

The Johnson family exchanged their gifts on Christmas Eve. Lady Bird's was especially personal and meaningful to the President—a bright red leather album of family Christmas photographs taken 1936–1964, together with a bronze plaque of the Inaugural medallion, featuring busts of the President and Vice President Hubert Humphrey. Many of the photographs Lady Bird had taken herself, so that her own gift from Lyndon was most appropriate: it was a movie camera.

Lynda Bird's gift to her parents was intriguing. It was a green leather album containing four eighteenth-century political cartoons by Hogarth.

Luci's gift to her father was a belt and gold buckle bearing the Presidential seal.

Willie Day Taylor, an old friend of the Johnsons from Amarillo, gave them two pecan trees to be planted beside the ranch.

From the eighty-five-year-old mother of J. C. Kellams, who manages the Johnsons' television interests, the President and his wife received homemade "patience candy."

From two-year-old Courtenay Lynda Valenti, daughter of a Presidential aide, the President received a tie and some handkerchiefs.

From Governor John Connally of Texas, the Johnsons received a pair of candlesticks made of pecan wood and fashioned after a pair owned by Texas's own Sam Houston. Mrs. W. Willard Wirtz, wife of the Secretary of Labor, sent them some candy.

On Christmas morning the President drove the First Lady and their elder daughter in his white Lincoln Continental to the little Episcopal Church of St. Barnabas, Fredericksburg, which Lady Bird loves. The President and Mrs. Johnson had laid the cornerstone of the building, which was completed with the latter's financial aid. An archway of roughhewn logs leads to the main doorway.

The First Family took Communion with the ever-present Secret Service man standing two steps behind them. He was Clint Hill, the man who hurled himself on the back of President Kennedy's limousine seconds after the fatal shots, perhaps saving Jacqueline Kennedy from assassination.

The President joined enthusiastically in the singing of "Joy to the World! The Saviour Comes," sharing Lynda Bird's hymnbook, his arm encircling her waist. As the congregation of about fifty sang "Hark! the Herald Angels Sing," Lynda Bird smiled into his face and slipped her arm around him.

St. Barnabas's vicar, the Reverend Jack W. Langford, stands three inches taller than the 6-foot-3-inch President. He prayed that "HIS peace, through us in the world, might bring peace to the nations . . . especially to Vietnam." Following the expiration of the thirty-hour truce, reports were already reaching the LBJ ranch of minor scattered Communist actions in that war-torn land.

As the First Family left the small picturesque church, the President asked a little boy how old he was.

"Eight, but I'll be nine next," was the prompt reply.

Christmas dinner at the ranch included the traditional turkey and sweet potatoes; then that afternoon Luci and Pat flew to Waukegan for a visit with his parents.

Arriving at Chicago's O'Hare International Airport aboard a Beechcraft Kingair private plane, they left by car for the Nugent family home, a two-story brick bungalow with gabled roof located on Waukegan's South Side, an area largely occupied by factory and steel millworkers of Lithuanian extraction. On Sunday they attended St. Bartholomew's Catholic Church, a radiant Luci wearing a large Christmas corsage.

While Pat and Luci were visiting in Waukegan, Lyndon and Lady Bird Johnson made a sentimental visit to his boyhood home in Johnson City to attend the First Baptist Church where his mother, the late Rebekah Baines Johnson, had worshiped. The pastor, the Reverend Howard L. McLerran, welcomed the Johnsons, describing Rebekah as "a lovely and gracious lady—a Bible-loving Baptist." He made a point of recalling in his sermon that other members of the Johnson and Baines families had long played a prominent role in Texas's Baptist life.

Afterward there was much handshaking, reunions with old friends, and greetings for visitors. The President has always showed how good he is with children and old folks. One elderly man called out, "Keep up Medicare."

The pastor took note of the larger-than-usual congregation, commenting with tongue in cheek that he hoped everyone had come that morning to hear him preach, then added that would be expecting too much.

Later, as the Johnsons drove up to the President's boyhood home, there was a security scare. Secret Service men spotted a young man standing close by holding a hunting rifle equipped with a telescopic sight. Simultaneously a little girl set off a loud firecracker.

A startled young hunter found himself the target of the Presidential bodyguard, who leapt from a security car and grabbed him. They soon discovered that Nicky Ammons, age eighteen, was leaving his own home near the old Johnson house to go deer hunting, and released him.

His basic training completed, Pat Nugent became a forty-hour-a-week airman with ten weeks of active clerical duty with the District of Columbia Air National Guard at Andrews Air Force Base, Maryland. During April he was released from this tour of active duty, after which he continued to take his military training one weekend a month with the 113th Tactical Fighter Squadron of the District of Columbia Guard.

On Saturday, February 12, 1966, Luci and Pat were honored by their first big post-engagement party at the exclusive City Tavern Club in Georgetown. Pat's parents were houseguests at theWhite House, meeting the Johnsons for the first time. Four of Luci's Texan friends were also houseguests: Bill Hitchcock and Ann Pittman of Austin, and Jim and Susan Ray of Hale Center.

The bride-to-be's close friend, debutante Helene Lindow, age eighteen, a Bennett College freshman, and her parents, Lester Lindow, a television executive, and Mrs. Lindow, arranged the party which had a hearts-and-flowers Valentine theme. Elizabeth Carpenter described the Nugents as "warm, wonderful people" and revealed that "they hit it off beautifully" with the Johnsons. The President of the United States was detained by official buiness elsewhere but arrived at the party following dinner.

Jerry Nugent, a registered Republican, had this to say of his visit to the White House: "We didn't discuss anything except our children. I wouldn't presume to talk to the President about anything else." Both Mrs. Nugent—Tillie— and he were delighted with the informality of their reception, noting that the First Lady quickly made them all feel like one big family. With her usual friendliness Lady Bird had quickly put the visitors at ease.

Lady Bird arrived with the Nugents and the betrothed couple in a White House limousine. Luci had personally chosen the 125 guests, many family friends and White House staffers being included. Sidney's Society Orchestra provided the music for the dancing, while pink topiary trees decorated with pink hearts and roses stood in silver pots upon the tables.

The following Monday it was announced that the wedding would take place not in the White House but in the National Shrine of the Immaculate Conception in Washington. Elizabeth Carpenter said that the Nuptial Mass would be offered by Archbishop Patrick O'Boyle and the Reverend John Kuzinskas, who was then assistant pastor of St. George's Church, Chicago, a lifetime friend of the Nugent family.

The Shrine, the largest Roman Catholic Church in the United States and the seventh largest in the world, is located on the campus of Catholic University. Built of limestone in the Byzantine and Romanesque styles, with a striking blue dome, it has thirty-five altars and can seat 3,500 people. Noting that the middle aisle is longer than a football field (348 feet), one aide quipped: "If the President and Luci make the trek down that aisle in ten minutes, it will only be because the President doesn't stop to shake hands with his friends."

Many girls' heads might well have been turned at the prospect of being married in the historic setting of the First House in the nation, yet Luci Johnson preferred a ceremony in the House of God.

"The emphasis will be on a family occasion," explained Elizabeth Carpenter. The ceremony would be followed by a reception in the White House.

Shortly afterward, Luci, who likes to cook, said that she intended to live upon her husband-to-be's income because he wouldn't hear of her going out to work. She said that she was definitely returning to nursing school next year, and that Pat would likewise continue his education, but that she would always have her nursing training to fall back on if times were "tough." She had talked budgets with Pat and had saved the $2-an-hour salary earned while she was working for the Washington optometrist.

Like all mothers, the First Lady declared that she wanted Luci to have a wedding to remember always as "a dream come true." Her daughter would be missed in the White House home where, according to Lady Bird, she was always "a sprite and a delight. . . . If we have any troubles, she comes in and cheers us up. . . . She's a determined little girl; a soft exterior belies a pretty strong character and she has the strength and ability to cope with life."

This last was the answer to the question with which

many mothers are posed due to the present trend of teen-age brides. "I think any parent would prefer a child to finish her education," said Lady Bird, "but on the other hand I think a year of planning it and a year of being sure about it is a very reasonable approach, and I do think Luci is a very feminine, domestic sort of girl for whom this will be right." In any case Luci was "happy as a lark" planning her wedding.

Lady Bird told the delightful story of Luci as "a little, bitty girl" who was told to limit her birthday party to "just best friends" as an illustration for what she was up against in choosing bridal attendants. The child Luci had replied, "But Mother, I have so many best friends."

"There are quite a few girls who have shared her life," reminisced the First Lady.

Speaking of the wedding, she said, "I want it to be as personal and as sentimental and as really hers and the family's as our life permits." She spoke as earnestly as any other mother wishing the best for her child.

The church selected for the ceremony was chosen not for size, as some Johnson critics had hinted, but "because it was a church she and Pat have gone to a lot and she has an attachment for it."

Clearing a First Lady's official calendar for the months of June and July was not easy, but Lady Bird wished to devote her time "to my personal life—to try to put together a lovely day to remember—the dream of every girl."

With remarkable restraint, a poised and smiling Luci weathered the blaze of publicity during the months imme-diately preceding her marriage. When asked the inevitable questions as to intimate wedding details she kept strictly mum. Good-naturedly she would speak out concerning the problems of being a President's daughter. Said Luci, "We don't get paid, but we sure get criticized."

After her engagement to Patrick Nugent, Luci seemed to

mature overnight. Most surprising were the strides she made in the world of fashion. No teen-ager ever had to swallow more sarcastic comments over her looks and figure than Luci Johnson. Her clothes were compared with those of Jacqueline Kennedy—and what teen-ager could hope to compare with a national institution! She was dubbed a "Texas schoolgirl," "a typical 4-H girl," and, worst of all to a girl about to leave the age of adolescence, "the corn-fed type." If she wore a more elaborate hairdo than usual, even the Secret Service agents would tease her with "Here comes Miss Teen-age Grandmother." Whenever Luci got mad with anyone she seemed to bake them a cake and all would be peaceful once more. She baked cakes for the agents . . . while, in addition to a cake, her father would get a poem.

Luci is much prettier than many of her pictures would have one believe, yet beauty did not come easy. Strict dieting with only an apple for lunch reduced her from 13 to size 8; a small bone structure inherited from her mother is now seen to advantage. Her fashion image improved to the point that women editors began to speculate if she would not one day make the Best Dressed list.

Patrick prefers light, delicate colors, and to please him Luci gave up wearing dark dresses. He also prefers clothes designed on simple lines which suit Luci's new model-like figure to perfection.

Fortunately, Luci while craving individuality in what she wears still takes direction. Luci, as other teen-agers, has in the past shopped more for a "look" than a "designer." Now Lady Bird has shown her how certain designers accent particular "looks." By studying these the customer can emerge with a specific fashion image.

Lady Bird invited both Adele Simpson and Mollie Parnis to display their collections to her daughters at a private showing in New York. Luci and Lynda Bird enjoyed themselves immensely. What a pleasure it was to look at clothes without being pestered by autograph hunters as they are when similarly engaged in the stores!

Following her engagement, Luci discovered three fashion principles. First, she learned to avoid fads; that Patrick was right when he preferred her wearing svelte tailored outfits created from quality fabrics. Secondly, she found that the shift-designed dresses so beloved by Mrs. Kennedy have become a classic in themselves. Luci enjoys the freedom of such unfitted garments. Seldom now, except for occasional evening wear, is she seen in form-clinging gowns. Thirdly, she has learned the value of wearing costumes, especially suits with coordinating blouses. The "rightness" of a matching coat she has finally mastered.

In the White House solarium, where President Truman once played poker and President Eisenhower made beef stews for his friends, Patrick, wearing shirt, Madras shorts, and white gym socks (no shoes), watched Luci as she described a dress hanging on the door. "She buys all her clothes at Robert Hall," he quipped.

Lady Bird and Luci shopped for the latter's trousseau in the privacy of a suite at the Hotel Carlyle in New York City. Attended by Lynda Bird, they quietly made their choices while designers and their assistants hurried in and out of the elevators, pursued by waiting reporters. But the designers and their VIP clients religiously kept silence. "Imagine," said Lady Bird triumphantly as she finally left for Washington, "three days in New York and nobody knows our secrets!"

One young man who turned up at the Hotel Carlyle during the Johnson ladies' visit was John-John Kennedy, son of the late President, who only wanted to get his English-style haircut in the hotel barbershop. Recognized by the host of photographers, he and his Nanny quickly disappeared into a nearby shoe store, where he was quite upset when he had to have red sandals instead of tan. As soon as Mrs. Johnson, her daughters, and the photographers had departed, John-John was settled in the barber chair reading up on Donald Duck.

As the wedding day grew close Lady Bird requested that the number of prenuptial parties being given for Luci and Patrick be curtailed as she felt that August 6 should be "the most wonderful day in her [Luci's] life." She didn't want Luci to spend the summer in a frantic effort to keep up with the whirl of party activities. Besides, the White House found that the wedding was "becoming more of a spectacular than Mrs. Johnson and Luci feel it ought to be." With the fighting in Vietnam, the White House was already sensitive to criticism of festive parties, held in the Executive Mansion and elsewhere, attended by members of the Administration.

Elizabeth Carpenter explained that "about five or six parties" were affected by Mrs. Johnson's request. One party allowed to proceed was that attended by some 125 of Luci and Patrick's friends from Milwaukee, where he had attended Marquette University, and from his hometown of Waukegan, given by dress manufacturer William Feldstein and Mrs. Feldstein at Milwaukee's plush Athletic Club. Luci had been the Feldsteins' guest when she visited Milwaukee to attend an LBJ barbecue meeting aimed at winning young voters for the Democratic ticket.

A curtailed party was a rooftop one to be given at one of Washington's best hotels by Mrs. Edmund Howar, whose daughter Bedar Howar, five, had already been announced as Luci's flower girl.

Meanwhile the Reverend John Kuzinskas, an assistant pastor of the Church of the Nativity of the Blessed Virgin

Mary, Chicago, family friend of the Nugents who would assist in the wedding ceremony said: "The wedding hasn't excited me yet. . . . Oh, it's natural there'll be a certain amount of tension at the time. But then, maybe not."

Now in his forties, as a teen-ager Father Kuzinskas had been a next-door neighbor of the Nugents. Often he had baby-sat for Patrick. When, years later, the "baby" was going out with Luci Johnson, Mrs. Nugent asked him if he could find out just how serious the romance was. Explained Father Kuzinskas, a genial outgoing man: "There hadn't been much time for Pat to talk with his family, and whenever anyone else brought up the question with Pat and Luci, they just changed the subject. So one day I asked Pat about it, and he said they were serious."

"My gosh, it can't be serious," had been the priest's reply. "I mean, she's still got four years of college to go. Give it some thought. Circulate around a bit."

The advice was not followed, and today Father Kuzinskas is far from sorry. Speaking of Luci, he says: "Her outlook on life and intellectuality are far more mature than anyone could expect. . . . She is a wonderful person, exuberant yet mature." Of Patrick, he adds: "There must be a lot of tension for him. There's a lot of scrutiny and he has to watch himself. But all the excitement and association in high places haven't turned his head."

During June, Luci spent a few days baby-sitting at the White House where she minded one-year-old Phyllis Montelaro, daughter of Mrs. and Mrs. James Montelaro. Phyllis's mother was in the hospital, where she gave birth to a little boy. Luci enjoyed looking after Phyllis immensely, proving once more just how excellent she is with youngsters.

The same month, with Patrick, she attended as guest of

honor the convention of the American Optometric Association auxiliary held in Boston, where she was promptly dubbed by an enthusiastic audience "the Unsinkable Luci."

Luci and her fiancé made quite a stir in proper Boston although there were some who were disappointed she did not dance the Watusi—a feat that seems fated for posterity like Princess Margaret's dancing the cancan.

"I came here for the optometrists' meeting, for nothing else," Luci kept repeating when pressed for details of her bridesmaids' dresses.

Luci is a good speaker, especially when she is interested in what she is talking about, and the subject of improving vision is close to her heart. Once suffering from esophoria —"My eyes were always fighting each other"—Luci could say with honesty: "I want to be more than honorary chairman. [She is chairman of Volunteers For Vision.] I want to be a real chairman. When my eye difficulty was corrected, my whole life was changed by being expanded into a greater life of variety." Patrick glowed as Luci returned twice to the podium to make further observations.

At the association's grand banquet held in the Hotel Sheraton-Boston, Luci wore a truly regal gown of sheer white chiffon with a long turquoise shawl. The band played "Deep in the Heart of Texas" in her honor and an Air Force song for Patrick.

Best compliment for the President's daughter came from the many Boston mothers who approved of her not wearing thigh-high hemlines. "But the President's daughter doesn't wear *her* skirts that short!" no doubt became a frequent admonition to their own children.

When Luci lunched beside Mrs. Richard Whitfield of Franklinton, N.C., outgoing president of the Association's auxiliary, she was asked about her mother. "Mother is just as busy as ever," was Luci's prompt reply.

Said Mrs. Whitfield afterward, "You'd think being the President's daughter, she might be snooty, but she wasn't a bit."

By mid-June, gifts for Luci and Patrick were beginning to pour in from all parts of the country—ranging from things old, new, borrowed, or blue to three sixpence to put in her shoe. Willie Day Taylor, a Johnson family friend and employee, had the job of cataloging everything. The White House solarium and Luci's bedroom both took on the appearance of a well-stocked department store.

The biggest category of gifts were handmade handkerchiefs, of which by June 15 Luci had already received more than fifty, mostly from elderly ladies. At that time she was getting 225 letters of congratulations and 50 gifts each week. There were crocheted pillowcases and sheets, nonstick cooking pans, a family Bible, religious figures, recipe books, patchwork quilts, and even a memory candle to burn on her Golden Wedding anniversary.

The homemade gifts touched Luci most of all, particularly the white cotton apron with a red heart-shaped pocket made by a fellow teen-ager.

Gifts from commercial concerns were declined and returned. Those from strangers costing more than ten dollars were also sent "gently" back, for Luci has always loved the little things in life best of all.

Luci's wedding cake was to be a summer fruitcake because, according to Mary Kaltman, White House food co-ordinator and executive housekeeper, it allowed Ferdinand Louvat, the White House pastry chef, to prepare it several weeks before the wedding day.

Ferdinand, a native of Grenoble, France, had been pastry chef at the Executive Mansion since April 1962. During his official baking career he had made over three hundred wedding cakes. He also baked the pastries for Queen Elizabeth's visit to France in 1957.

The Gothic-style cake had thirteen layers, including a smaller chocolate cake on top made from the recipe of Mrs. Roy Folk Beal of Austin, Texas, mother of Betty Beal, one of Luci's bridesmaids. This tiny chocolate "honeymoon cake" was in fact taken by the newlyweds on their honeymoon.

The cake, iced with white fondant, was decorated with sugar swans, roses, and lilies of the valley. Real lilies of the valley replaced the usual model bride and groom on top.

Here is Luci's wedding cake recipe in home-size instead of White House proportions:

"Cover ½ cup of white seedless raisins with apple juice and place in the refrigerator for two or three days or until the raisins are plump. Drain and spread on a towel to dry surface moisture. To 1¾ cups of sifted flour, add 1 teaspoon of double-acting baking powder and ¼ teaspoon of salt and sift together three times. Cream ½ cup of butter thoroughly and add ¾ cup of sugar gradually. Cream together until light and fluffy. Add 5 unbeaten egg whites, one at a time, beating thoroughly after each. Add ¾ cup of chopped candied pineapple, 1 cup of chopped pecans, the soaked raisins, ½ teaspoon of almond extract, and ½ teaspoon of vanilla extract, and mix well.

Add the flour mixture a little at a time, carefully beating after each addition until smooth.

Bake in a low oven (300°) in a loaf pan which has been greased, lined with heavy paper, and greased again. (The loaf pan should measure 8 by 4 by 3 inches.) Bake the cake about 1¼ hours.

It is interesting to compare this Presidential wedding cake recipe with that baked for Martha Wayles Skelton when she married Thomas Jefferson at "The Forest," her

father's home in Charles City County, west of Williamsburg, Virginia, on January 1, 1772.

The Jefferson wedding cake was rich and black, containing 20 eggs, 2 pounds of powdered sugar, 2 pounds of
butter, 2½ pounds of the best white flour, 5 pounds of
fruit, ½ pint of wine, ¼ ounce of mace, 1 ounce of nut-
meg and some French brandy. It was slowly baked for 5
hours.

Shopping together in Georgetown, Pat and Luci chose
Ceralene's Ambassador dinner service because they were
fascinated with the practical, straight-sided cups. Kirk's
engraved Old Maryland flat silver was picked to compliment the gold-bordered dinner plates.

As the wedding day approached, like any other bride,
Luci was nervous. "I'm not just nervous," she said, "I'm
happy, excited, filled with hopes, dreams, desires—a con-
glomeration of emotions, including a little bit of apprehen-
sion and a great deal of happiness." To this her father
added that he was "awfully glad to be getting a son at
last."

The ceremony was announced as being a "family affair"
and not a state occasion which eliminated head-of-state
protocol and invitations to everyone of importance in the
diplomatic community. The 700 invited guests were mostly
family friends. After much soul searching the family decided that the actual ceremony should not be televised.
Helen Lindow, eighteen, one of the bridesmaids, viewed
the prospect of walking in the long bridal procession as "a
little scary."

Luci's wedding invitations were engraved in hand-cut
script upon an Ecru white (cream-colored) paper. Like
similar invitations of other Presidential-daughter brides, the
Presidential coat of arms was embossed at the center top of
the invitation. Measuring 6 by 9 inches, they read:

> *The President and Mrs. Johnson*
> *request the honour of your presence*
> *at the marriage of their daughter*
> *Luci Baines*
> *to*
> *Mr. Patrick John Nugent*
> *on Saturday the sixth of August*
> *one thousand nine hundred and sixty-six*
> *at twelve o'clock noon*
> *The National Shrine of the Immaculate Conception*
> *in the city of Washington*

The smaller reception card read:

> *Following the ceremony*
> *a reception will be held at*
> *The White House*

Luci herself ended the controversy over a gift she had not solicited from the members of Congress. Democratic leader Carl Albert of Oklahoma had been designated keeper of a wedding gift fund by Speaker John W. Mc-Cormack (Democrat, Massachusetts) and GOP leader Gerald R. Ford of Michigan.

The plan had been launched by a "Dear Colleague" letter from McCormack and Ford saying, "It is our thought and suggestion that it would be highly appropriate for members of the House to join together in presenting a wedding gift to Luci Baines Johnson and her fiancé."

The suggestion was sourly received by Representative H. R. Gross (Republican, Iowa), who announced, "Personally, I'm not about to buy a wedding present for one of the heiresses to a seventeen-million-dollar monopoly fortune."

With simple dignity Luci settled the matter of the bipartisan gift when she said, "I treasure my family's friends in

Congress, but I hope that no contribution will be accepted for any present for us."

The President also politely endeavored to refuse official gifts and delegations for the wedding. Prime Minister Indira Gandhi's offer of a present from her government was delicately declined, and one royal family was asked not to send a representative. A silver tea service from the Washington diplomatic corps was, however, accepted.

When *Women's Wear Daily*, a fashion trade newspaper, prematurely released embargoed news material on the bridesmaids' gowns, the White House announced that working press credentials would be denied it for the actual wedding. When women reporters asked Elizabeth Carpenter if there would be telephones in their church pews, she retorted, "It's strictly on your knees, girls, for ninety minutes." Shouldering much of the load of the wedding arrangements, jovial Mrs. Carpenter quipped weeks before the actual day, "It's going to be a long, hot summer with rioting in the East Wing." For anybody unethical enough to jump her press release dates giving wedding information, she assured them that "A large guillotine will be erected on the South Lawn for minor offenders." For the benefit of those editors who had followed her dicta, she expressed her "appreciation to all media that have cooperated on the wedding-story release date in the high tradition of American journalism."

Less than three weeks before the actual wedding day, Luci sat with her mother upon a beige settee in the State Dining Room to talk with women reporters. A portrait of Abraham Lincoln by George Peter Alexander Healy (1813–1892) looked benignly down on the scene. Luci, who was wearing a short pink-and-white gingham cotton outfit, was poised and ready with her answers.

"If you have a son, would you want him to grow up and be President of the United States?" one reporter asked her.

"Well," answered Luci, after carefully weighing the matter for a few moments, "if I ever have a son, I want the same thing for him that my parents have given me, and that is a chance to be the best of what I have to offer. My family has never given me too rigid guidelines. They have set down some standards they believed in and we have worked together and they let me develop in my own mind what is the best for me. So that is what I want for my son. Whatever talent or interest he has, I would want him to pursue it."

The bride-to-be sipped pink lemonade as she talked, while every now and then her mother gave a little smile of encouragement.

"I will miss those late-night talks and so many things that we share," confessed the First Lady.

Luci then thanked the reporters who had each brought her a recipe for her cookbook. She corrected the impression that she could only cook fried chicken and brownies. "I am rather versatile," said she. "I have a lot to learn, and from all the recipes you brought today I'm sure I have a lot to learn. I am by no means an accomplished, great cook, but I can put on a different meal for two main meals seven days a week without having a duplicate!"

Asked if she would not expect her new husband to wash and dry the dishes, she replied most emphatically: "If he wanted to help, I don't think I would refuse. But no, I plan to take care of the household, to the best of my ability."

Admitting that she missed Patrick, who was away on two weeks of National Guard duty in Georgia, "like a front tooth," Luci then revealed what had most attracted her to the young man from Waukegan: "He is a very honest person, a very sincere person, a very religious person. . . . Our marriage can only survive and grow through our religion. Because we feel the same way about our religion, we feel that we will grow closer together and appreciate more in life as a result of that common bond."

Luci, like other brides, was quick to admit that the hardest thing for her will be leaving the family. "I have always stayed home and been around my mother and father. . . . It is difficult to know that things won't be the same in many aspects. . . . What will I miss most? My parents. Then the people I've come to love here and of course my dogs. They really belong to me but they've given Daddy so much pleasure I couldn't take them with me."

Lady Bird was then asked if she had any advice for making a marriage work. "I am not in the advice-giving business," she answered with a smile, "but if I were, I think I would just say that to remember each day is a new day, to be lived fresh and enjoyed to the utmost. Put the most into it that you can to help the person you are with, and share it with him. Just keep alive lots and lots of interests."

To which Luci added: "You feel very owned, very possessed, when you're getting married. Every bride has to learn it's not her wedding but her mother's!

"We don't want this wedding to be a spectacular," she added. "We're not royalty. It's not a state occasion. . . . You know, I'm marrying a man I've never been out with alone."

The wedding week was marked by parties and gaiety. Former New York Governor Averell Harriman and Mrs. Harriman entertained members of the Diplomatic Corps in honor of Luci and Pat, and the President attended. Most informal was a Texas-style cookout held two days before the wedding and hosted by Steve Steinert of Charleston, South Carolina, and William B. Hitchcock, III, and Stafford Hutchinson, both of Austin, Texas. It rained so hard during the evening that the bales of hay substituting for chairs were deserted for dryer spots indoors. The party was held at Hutchinson's home in Westmoreland Hills, Maryland. Luci and Lynda Bird gaily set the pace with their party finery—the bride-to-be in a red-and-white polka-dot blouse and hip-huggers, her sister in a green flowered sunsuit and green sunglasses. "It was wonderful," exclaimed the sentimental Luci afterward. "I really appreciated this last opportunity to get together with my friends."

Pat's "bachelor party" turned out instead to be an exhibition professional football game held in the D.C. Stadium. Instead of an elaborate dinner there were hamburgers and soft drinks afterward.

Luci's twelve bridal attendants were each given a gold bracelet with a circular gold charm decorated with a floral bouquet of gold in the center and seven small deep-pink rubies. On the reverse side was engraved the attendant's name and the message, "A bouquet of friendship and love, Luci," together with the wedding date.

Pat gave his groomsmen sterling silver money clips with their intitials and the engraving, "Pat and Luci, August 6, 1966."

Mrs. Alice Wilson McElroy, a niece of President Woodrow Wilson who was married in the White House on August 7, 1918, forty-eight years almost to the day before Luci Johnson's wedding, supplied Luci with a small gold bar pin worn at her own wedding for "something borrowed." Mrs. McElroy, wife of the Reverend I. S. McElroy, Jr., told newsmen that she was happy that Luci was being married in a church instead of in the White House. She related a delightful anecdote of the McElroy wedding to reporters, of how the bridegroom lost his suspenders and had to borrow safety pins and a belt from the President.

There were large crowds on hand outside of the Shrine of the Immaculate Conception—larger than on the wedding day itself—for the wedding rehearsal. The President led Luci, who was wearing a bedsheet in place of her train, down the long aisle. He was happy and talkative. "I've always wanted a boy," he said. "We're getting the kind of boy we like and wanted. Luci is a happy, bouncy, and lively girl. We're very happy." Previously he had confessed: "You know, I'm looking forward to Pat's company and occasionally his support in family discussions. I've always been outnumbered up till now."

Lady Bird described the rehearsal as "beautiful."

Back at the White House six of Luci's attendants—including her sister-in-law to be, Mrs. Gerard Nugent, Jr., of San Diego, California—were houseguests.

The wedding morning was warm and sunny—a typical Washington August day. For once there were no crowds of tourists as the Executive Mansion had been closed to the general public for the day. To make up for this, Luci had requested that the house should be open on Monday, a day that it is normally closed.

The President, who had refused to wear a formal cutaway at his inauguration ceremonies, bowed to Luci's wishes and wore one for the wedding. Even on their way to the church the First Family were not allowed to forget Vietnam, for they had to pass a group of pickets protesting both the war and the fact that August 6 was the twenty-first anniversary of the atomic bombing of Hiroshima.

Lady Bird, whose composure throughout the ceremony was much commented upon, was wearing an ensemble of a lemon sherbet shade with a turban hat. She looked more like an elder sister of the bride than her mother.

Luci, with her full-length bridal grown of pure white lace with a ten-foot-long train hanging from the shoulders, looked truly regal. It was hard to visualise in that sleek, trim figure the robust teen-ager of a few years back. Her veil and headdress arrangement was particularly suited to her features, the veil framing the face somewhat like an eighteenth-century calash. When Lady Bird had first seen the bridal gown she described it as being "the kind you would hand down to your grandchildren." She regretted not having had a wedding gown herself that she could let her daughter wear. So that Luci's gown could become a family heirloom, the bride's name and wedding date were embroidered into the hemline.

The lilies of the valley for Luci's tiny bouquet had been specially grown at the White House. Actually there were two identical bouquets, as the bridal pair later placed one before the statue of St. Agatha, Patron Saint of Nursing.

For a short time it seemed that the worries and cares that beset the President of the United States and his First Lady were laid aside as the father of the bride walked slowly down the 400-foot-long aisle with Luci upon his arm. It was a long walk for any man to have to take to "give away" a much-loved daughter. As one usher noted, "He had a sort of wistful look—unhappy and proud at the same time." When they reached the foot of the altar steps where Pat was waiting to escort Luci the rest of the way, Luci seemed for a brief moment to sense her father's momentary loneliness. Quietly she placed her hand upon his shoulder in a gesture of farewell and then, an apparition of shimmering white, she was gone.

The Nuptial Mass incorporated many of the innovations of the Catholic Liturgy as approved by the recent Vatican Council. "May the God of Israel join you together; and may He be with you" sang the combined choirs from the Cathedral of Mary Our Queen and the Church of the Immaculate Heart of Mary, both in Baltimore. Robert F. Twynham, who played the organ, wrote original music for sections of the Mass, substituting his own arrangements. "Paraphrase on a Trumpet Tune," for a more familiar wedding march. Norman Sydor directed the joint choirs of men and boys numbering approximately a hundred voices.

The enormous shrine is not air-conditioned. It stands high upon a hill, overlooking the capital city, and normally the thick stone walls tend to keep it cool. During the cere-

mony there seemed little cross ventilation. As maid of
honor, Lynda Bird, noticeably more nervous than the
bride, was standing close to the immediate wedding party.
Suddenly she slumped forward. Three priests went to her
aid and a chair was provided.

Lynda Bird and the other attendants wore floor-length
Empire-style gowns in various shades of pink moire, called
for the occasion "August Pinks." Designed by Priscilla of
Boston (Priscilla Kidder, who found fame in the fashion
world when she designed the wedding and bridesmaids'
gowns for Grace Kelly, now Princess Grace of Monaco),
they were offset by pink illusion veiling that fell like medie-
val headdresses from the back of the attendants' high hair-
dos clear to the floor.

The little flower girl, Bedar Howar, had no long veil.
Lyndon "Corky" Hand, the ring bearer, wore a neat suit
with short pants. As the President's godson, he called the
bride "Aunt Luci" and revealed, "She was a good baby
sitter."

While Luci's "I do" was firm, Pat's was soft. There were
tears in his eyes and he brushed them away. There were
three rings: one for Pat and two diamond-studded bands
for Luci, one to wear on either side of her engagement
ring. Pat's father stood proxy as best man for his elder son,
Gerard, Jr., on active duty in Vietnam. The bridegroom's
parents are both surprisingly youthful-looking. Pat's
mother, dressed in a pretty shade of blue, had said earlier
in the week when the couple arrived in Washington, "I'm
not nervous, and I'm not going to be all week."

At 12:42 Luci Baines Johnson was officially Mrs. Patrick Nugent. At last she had some initials of her own instead of the LBJ she had shared with the rest of her family
all her life. As the Mass ended and the newlyweds walked
slowly down the aisle toward the main door, bells in the
giant carillon, played by Robert Grogan, pealed out from

the two belfries set in the slender bell tower 329 feet above the ground. It was a fitting climax to the wedding of a President's daughter.

Lynda Bird carried the flowing train and how well she did it! International reporters recalled the mixup in the carrying of the bridal train of Crown Princess Beatrix of the Netherlands.

Following the happy couple came the bride's parents. Lyndon had Lady Bird's arm gripped firmly in his as if he were afraid of losing her in the crowd, while she greeted numerous friends by name. It wasn't until they were outside the Shrine that she was able to extract her arm and then gently entwine it again with Lyndon's. Back at the White House the President himself helped Tillie Nugent from her car and placed an encouraging arm upon her shoulder. Several days before he had somewhat prematurely described Pat as "my son-in-law."

Among the guests who were enthusiastic about the service were Senate Republican Leader Everett M. Dirksen of Illinois, and Mrs. Dirksen, who praised the wedding leaflet, which explained each section of the Mass in detail. Supreme Court Justice William O. Douglas was there with his fourth bride, who was delighted with her first visit to Washington.

Peter Duchin's orchestra welcomed all the guests from the church to the reception, for, as Lady Bird had explained, her hospitable Texas nature was offended by the thought of asking them to the ceremony and not to the White House afterward. First thing on Mrs. Patrick Nugent's agenda was to visit her dogs. Her large white collie Blanco was particularly loving, as Luci in her long veil knelt down to embrace him. Pat, who also loves dogs, was surrounded by a collection of beagles. As the newlyweds re-entered the White House, Pat exclaimed, "I've never seen so many newspaper people in my life."

Outside both the Shrine and the White House, the crowds were remarkably restrained and well behaved in contrast to the moblike behavior of those outside the Newport, Rhode Island, church a few days previously for the wedding of Jacqueline Kennedy's half-sister, Janet Auchincloss. Women had screamed, "There she is!" when the former First Lady appeared; children provoked the page-boy John-John by shouting "Sissy" at him . . . and the bewildered bride just cried.

The only hitch in the entire wedding proceedings occurred during the cutting of the wedding cake in the gold and white East Room. First the bride and groom mounted the special platform for the ceremonial slicing of the thirteen-tier cake, but try as they would, the silver knife would not crack through the hard white icing. It provided some hilarious relief to a tension-filled day. After what seemed to be an eternity of determined sawing they switched to another layer and yet another. . . . Finally the fourth layer yielded to the young Nugents' determined onslaught.

The top chocolate layer they later took on their honeymoon. Each guest was given tiny "favor" cakes packed in white heart-shaped satin boxes. Among the telegrams of good wishes received was one from Jack Benny, the comedian, up until that time Waukegan's most famous son.

Later Mr. and Mrs. Patrick Nugent left for a secret honeymoon in Nassau, the Bahamas, before setting up housekeeping in half of a new two-family duplex at 1105 Heritage Way, Austin, Texas, which rents for approximately $165 a month, and according to Luci has "two skylights, which I find just great, and besides, they save electricity."

Their new home has a cathedral ceiling in the living room, two bedrooms, two bathrooms, and a modern kitchen complete with automatic dishwasher. The couple had so many gifts for their home that Luci said her parents had given her a savings bond of an undisclosed sum, as there was nothing else she needed.

Pat's favorite meal is fried chicken. The following is Luci's menu for one of her first suppers cooked in their new home:

Green Salad. Select choice pieces of washed and chilled Boston, Bibb, iceberg, and romaine lettuce and arrange in bowl with young broccoli stalks sliced into spears and steamed until tender, then marinated in lemon and oil. Top with sliced and peeled cucumbers and small celery sticks, salt, pepper, and French dressing.

Fried Chicken. Cut chicken into pieces, allowing one fryer per person. First wash and then dry sections between paper towels. Mix flour, salt, and pepper in paper bag, then shake chicken pieces inside until coated. Place in black iron skillets with 1½ fingers high of hot fat. Turn with fork for 5 to 10 minutes until browned. Cover loosely, then brown on low heat for 20 minutes, occasionally turning. Uncover, then continue cooking until chicken is well-browned, crisp, and done. Turn occasionally. Drain on paper towels, then serve with slices of French bread spread with soft butter, then fried in heavy iron skillet with more butter until golden brown and crisp.

Lemon Cake. Sift 1¼ cups of sugar, then gradually beat into ¾ cup of soft, lightly salted butter. Beat until light and creamy. In a separate bowl beat 8 egg yolks until light and lemon-colored, then blend into the butter-sugar mixture. Sift together three times 2½ cups of sifted cake flour, 3 teaspoons of baking powder, ¼ teaspoon of salt; add to the butter-sugar mixture in three parts, alternating with thirds of ¾ cup of milk. After each addition beat thoroughly. Then add and beat for 2 minutes each: 1 teaspoon each of lemon juice, vanilla, and lemon rind. Bake in two greased,

9-inch layer pans for 20 minutes, or until properly done, at 375° F. Spread with lemon icing and sprinkle with grated lemon rind. For icing: blend well 2 cups of confectioners' sugar, ¼ cup of soft butter. Beat in the grated rind and juice of 1 lemon and 1 or more teaspoons of heavy cream.

6

Christmas Child

✳   ✳

I⊤ was a crisp wintry morning in Karnack, Texas, when Lady Bird was born in 1912. Christmas was only three days away and the servants had been speculating, as servants will, whether or not the baby would arrive on December twenty-fifth. She disappointed them, but when her Negro nurse called her "purty as a Lady Bird," all was forgiven.

Dr. Benjamin Baldwin, who had delivered the newcomer, warmed his tingling fingers—for it can be very cold at that time of the year, even in Texas—over one of the generous fires that burned in all the grates of the red brick mansion. Thomas Jefferson Taylor II, so big that he seemed naturally fitted for the courtesy title of "Cap," affectionately bestowed upon him by the neighbors, was elated that after two sons and an interval of eight years his pretty wife, Minnie Lee, had at last presented him with a daughter.

Cultured and intellectual, Minnie was the daughter of Luke Pattillo of Billingsley, Alabama, a man proud of his Scottish and Spanish background. The Taylors were of English descent, farming their own land nearby. Minnie

fell in love with bluff, amiable Tom after riding horseback
to his family's farm to meet him. They married despite the
objections of her family who, in common with their other
Alabaman neighbors, did not approve of Taylor methods
of farming.

Thomas Taylor could be described as a rough diamond
beside the tall, ethereal girl he made his bride; but, as often
is the case, opposites attract. Perhaps it was his great ambition that pleased her, for when Tom decided to leave Alabama to seek his fortune she did not hesitate to pack her
beloved books and accompany him. Family tradition has
the newlyweds so determined to try their luck in the raw
Texas country that they were scarcely out of the state of
Louisiana when they got off the train.

They settled near Karnack, a little town which, in spite
of the misspelling, was called after the famed Karnak ruins
in Upper Egypt. It was there that Tom Taylor was to have
his general store with the intriguing sign outside: T. J.
TAYLOR, DEALER IN EVERYTHING.

He proved to be an acute businessman. With the pro-
ceeds from his store, two cotton gins, and the land he was
to acquire over the years, he was able to keep his wife in
her accustomed style.

In Karnack, Minnie is remembered as "a cultured
woman" who "didn't consort with Karnack people." This
was putting it mildly, for in a country community where
the wives talked of church socials and preserves, Minnie
was a complete misfit. She was a studious woman whose
bookshelves would have done credit to a college professor.
In addition to the classics she enjoyed history, biography,
and the works of Voltaire, with H. Rider Haggard's writings on the occult thrown in for good measure.

As soon as Lady Bird—or Claudia Alta, which was her
real name—was barely able to understand she was introduced to the mysteries of Greek, Roman and German

mythology. She still insists that the legendary Siegfried, with his magic cloak and sword, was her first love.

Lady Bird's first five years were spent in a little world of extremes—the aesthetic and the monetary. While her mother played grand opera on the phonograph, her father rose at four each morning to open his store and bring in the dollars. Minnie was adored by her servants and criticized by the neighborhood for her "weird and stand-offish" practice of entertaining Negroes. She was intensely interested in Negro religious practices and once began to write a book which she titled *Bio Baptism*. Her liberal interests were not shared by her husband, although he does not seem to have objected to her having an open mind.

Minnie, who fussed over food and wore heavy veils, is recalled by Lady Bird as a "tall, graceful woman who wore white quite a lot and went around the house in a great rush." At one point she suffered a nervous breakdown and was in a Battle Creek, Michigan, hospital for some time, returning to Karnack after her recovery. Then, expecting another child, she was walking up the circular staircase when the family's collie dog rushed between her feet, causing her to lose her balance and fall to the bottom. A miscarriage resulted, followed by blood poisoning. Lady Bird, not yet six, was taken to see her mother in the county hospital, where on September 14, 1918, Minnie Lee Pattillo Taylor died. She was forty-four years old.

"My father was a strong man, to put it mildly," Lady Bird once said of Cap Taylor. "As I look back on Mother's death I am terrifically sorry for Daddy, and quite sorry for my two brothers. They were thirteen and sixteen at the time, and their lives were adversely affected by the sudden pulling away of a woman who would have seen that they received good educations. But I don't feel in the least sorry for myself. At five, one is pretty much insulated from pain.

Besides, I was quite sure that she was going to come back. I could hear people saying that Mother was gone. I could tell that they were feeling sorry for me, but I thought to myself, 'Well, I know more about that than they do. She'll be back.' But as time went on, I quit even thinking about it. It may have been some sort of protective cloak that nature puts around young folks, but I never thought of myself as having a lonely childhood."

Even if she was not conscious of being lonely, her adoring father thought that she might be, and his remedy was to take her to his beloved store each day. He put up a cot on the second floor and, when she inquired what the "row of peculiar long boxes" might be, her father said they were "dry goods." She later found out they were coffins.

The store was Lady Bird's first taste of the world of business—experience she later put to excellent use. Cotton was king in the Karnack country. She listened attentively when the farmers who sharecropped her father's acres discussed their problems in the store.

By the following Christmas Cap decided that running a business and bringing up a little girl single-handed did not go well together. Relatives came to the rescue, and he decided to accept their suggestion that his spinster sister-in-law, Effie Pattillo, was the best solution.

Aunt Effie responded by immediately entraining for Texas from her native Alabama. Like her older sister Minnie, Effie was well educated if just as unworldly. By the time Lady Bird was eight she had read *Ben Hur* by herself and could recite long, difficult poems that she remembers to this day. Just as Minnie had played grand opera on the phonograph, Effie loved to play the piano.

With her brothers, Tom III and Antonio, away at school, Lady Bird's only other young companions were the Negro children whose mothers worked in the big house. She listened avidly to their wonderful stories of ghosts and the unseen.

Aunt Effie would invent make-believe friends as they took long walks together through the woods and enjoyed the huge boughs of pine and the crape myrtle that bloomed in profusion as high as the second-story window of the room where Lady Bird was born. Through Aunt Effie's eyes Lady Bird came to love and know wildflowers and trees by name. Said the child who grew up to be First Lady: "She opened my spirit to beauty, but she neglected to give me any insight into the practical matters a girl should know about, such as how to dress or choose one's friends or learn to dance. . . . She was undoubtedly the most otherworldly human in the world. She was delicate and airy and very gentle, and she gave me many fine values which I wouldn't trade for the world. She had a polite musical education considered proper for a young lady of her day, and she played the piano quite well. She was, however, always thinking of others, and was a great hand to look after all the needy members of the family and the community."

Every summer, Lady Bird and Effie escaped the hot Texas sun by visiting relatives in Alabama or making trips as far afield as Colorado or Michigan. Reminiscing about her Alabama holidays, Mrs. Johnson recalled nostalgically: "I remember—who could ever forget?—the laughing hayrides and watermelon suppers, learning to swim in Mulberry Creek, the lazy curl of a cousin's fishing line flickering in the sun, church on Sunday and then the long Sunday dinner with kinsfolk—endless kinsfolk—discussing the endless family gossip around the table."

Claude Pattillo, Aunt Effie's bachelor brother, doted upon Lady Bird. Determined that she should one day attend Harvard Business School (she didn't), he made her read books on finance, and by the time she was twelve had her studying stock-market quotations with the eye of an expert. For Christmas he sent her books on property management and business methods, and Lady Bird loved to read them. Like Minnie, Claude was a food faddist, and he advised his niece always to watch her diet. When he died he left her vast interests in Alabama cotton and timber land.

Lady Bird's education began in a one-room school-house, once so much a part of the American scene. She particularly recalls Friday afternoons when the children sang patriotic songs they had learned by heart. The desks were arranged around "a plump stove" in the middle of the room, which on wintry mornings was lit by the bigger boys, whose job it was also to carry in the logs. Lady Bird studied there from the first grade through the seventh. She enjoyed telling her own daughters about it, especially how at one time she was the only child enrolled.

Although she regularly attended the local Methodist church with her family, she was often taken to the little Negro church with her nurse and Negro playmates. She had early inherited her mother's friendly understanding and found these services rich and exciting. She still loves to talk of her childhood, recalling, "I used an oil lamp until I was nine years old, and I can remember what a big day it was when we finally got indoor plumbing."

On completing elementary school Lady Bird studied in Jefferson for two years, where she shared an apartment with Aunt Effie. High school followed at Marshall, the county seat, eighteen miles from home. Aunt Effie might have been "out of this world" but she seems to have raised no objections when Cap allowed thirteen-year-old Lady Bird to drive her own car down the dirt road to high school and back.

The interest in her education taken by her mother, Aunt Effie, and Uncle Claude bore good results, for Lady Bird was an apt student. With a straight "Grade A" to her credit, it seemed that she might well get the best grades in her class and have to give either the valedictorian or saluta-torian address at graduation. Lady Bird was petrified, exclaiming she would "just as soon have the smallpox as open my mouth."

Happily for her, a close friend, Emma Boehringer, won the honor of valedictorian with an average of 95. Maurine Kranson with 94.5 would be the salutatorian. A much-relieved Lady Bird was third with 94!

She was now fifteen years old and, in those early teen years, rather a wallflower.

Said a former schoolmate, Mrs. Naomi Bell of Marshall: "Bird wasn't accepted into our clique. There were eighteen of us girls, and we couldn't get Claudia to cooperate on anything. She didn't date at all. To get her to go to the high school graduation banquet, my fiancé took Bird as his date and I went with another boy. She didn't like to be called Lady Bird, so we'd call her Bird to get her little temper going. My mother would call her Cat. She'd say, 'All right, pull your claws in, Cat.' And when the rest of the gang was in the house, Bird would sneak in the back door and talk to my mother. She was a chatterbox. But she was timid. When she got in a crowd, she'd clam up."

On leaving high school at Marshall, Lady Bird enrolled at St. Mary's School for Girls, in Dallas, a Protestant Episcopal junior college that resulted in her decision to become an Episcopalian. After graduating with an "A" average, she proceeded to the University of Texas in Austin. There, although she clung lovingly to her Aunt Effie's old coat, she drove her own Buick, had her own charge account, and the privilege of her father's checkbook—quite a combination in the days of the Depression. She also learned to dance the Louisiana Stomp.

In 1933 Lady Bird earned a Bachelor of Arts degree, then decided to stay on for another year in order to obtain one in journalism because she believed that journalists met such interesting people. As if these accomplishments were not enough, she obtained a second-grade teacher's certificate and learned how to qualify for a secretarial job, explaining, "Once you get your foot in the door as a good secretary, you can go places." Her ambition was to work in some far-off, romantic-sounding place such as Alaska or Hawaii.

According to her close friend Eugenia (Gene) Boehringer: "When we would talk about getting married, Bird would just say she wanted a nice man and a big white house with a fence around it and a big collie dog. She wanted a nice nine-to-five man. A John Citizen."

Lady Bird enjoyed her stay in Austin. "I fell in love with Austin the first moment that I laid eyes on it, and that love has never slackened."

Gene Boehringer was "one of those tremendously outgoing people who made everyone around her feel a little more alive," and life was never dull when Gene was there, for she always thought of exciting things to do. When Gene learned that Cap Taylor was giving Lady Bird a trip to Washington as a graduation present, she insisted that her Karnack friend must meet a certain young man who would show her the city.

Gene wrote his name on a piece of paper. It was Lyndon B. Johnson.

Lady Bird set out for the capital with her roommate, Cecile Harrison, but as they already knew several Texans living there, Lady Bird failed to call Lyndon, explaining, "I would have felt mighty odd calling an absolute stranger."

Then fate decided to step in. A few weeks later—in August 1934—Lyndon and Lady Bird met for the first time in Gene's office at the State Capitol building in Austin. He was twenty-six and she was twenty-one.

Although she thought him "excessively thin," Lady Bird noted his extreme good looks and thick black wavy hair. He was the most outspoken man she had ever encountered.

This was really the beginning of the magic combination

of Lyndon and Lady Bird that was to lead him, with her encouragement, to the highest office in the land.

"I knew I had met something remarkable, but I didn't quite know what," was her immediate reaction.

Dorothy Muckleroy, another friend, was also in the office. Lyndon took them all out for coffee. He seemed immediately attracted to the rather shy Lady Bird, whom Gene was always imploring to be more "outgoing." As he had already dated Dorothy for the evening, he compromised by asking Lady Bird to have breakfast with him at the Driskill Hotel dining room next morning. She accepted somewhat reluctantly. "I was uncertain whether I wanted to have breakfast with him, as I had a queer sort of moth-and-the-flame feeling about what a remarkable man he was."

Next morning she had an appointment with architect Hugo Kuehne in connection with the restoration of her family home which she had promised to superintend for her father. When she left Kuehne's office, which was next door to the hotel, Lyndon was watching for her out of the window. There was no escape. He has always thought she would never have had the courage to enter the dining room looking for him if he hadn't waylaid her.

After breakfast Lyndon suggested a drive, during which he told her "all sorts of things that I thought were extraordinarily direct for a first date." By the time he had returned her to Austin she felt caught up in a Texas tornado. She knew that he enjoyed his work as Congressional secretary to Representative Richard Kleberg, a part owner of the famous King Ranch; she knew how long he had been teaching before that, and just how much insurance he was carrying.

He had even managed to get Lady Bird to speak a little of herself and her ambitions; that Karnack held little future for an educated young woman.

Lyndon was fascinated. Right away, he wanted her to meet his parents. When that meeting took place, Lady Bird was quick to sense that Rebekah Baines Johnson idolized her eldest son, so that she could "almost see the uncertainty" in her eyes. Of his mother, Lyndon has said: "My mother was a saintly woman. I owe everything to her."

A graduate of Baylor College, Rebekah taught her son his alphabet from blocks before he was two years old. Lady Bird might have been raised upon *Ben Hur* and Greek mythology, but her husband-to-be at the age of three could recite all the Mother Goose rhymes in addition to some verses by Longfellow and Tennyson. At four he was reading short sentences, and when he eventually started school her coaching and interest at home spurred him on.

To make his own way through high school, Lyndon had shined shoes in a barbershop, and after graduation, with his mother's approval, he had set out "to see the world," working his way by washing dishes and waiting table all the way to California. When he hitchhiked home again to Johnson City he was thin as a rake.

"Education opens up everything," Rebekah now impressed upon her son, who had lost little time in getting a job as a laborer with a road gang. She finally persuaded him to enter Southwest Texas State Teachers' College—San Marcos in February 1927.

Lyndon (whom his fellow students nicknamed Bull), has called the San Marcos years "the most formative period in my life." Author Jack Bell notes ironically that Lyndon "got an early lesson in budget-balancing by borrowing $75 at the Johnson City bank to finance his matriculation at San Marcos. This was about the time that Joe Kennedy was settling a $1 million trust fund on his nine-year-old son John."

At college, Lyndon took a janitor's job which he hated so much that he was determined to obtain his degree as quickly as possible. He later earned $75 a month as editor-in-chief of the *College Star*, took forty courses, and made thirty-five A's. His great love was debating. Obtaining his degree in August 1930, he began teaching, taking a year from his own course to instruct seventeen pupils in the brick school at Cotulla, Texas. The monthly salary of $100 was enough to complete his own education.

Knowing all this, Lady Bird understood the feelings of this older woman who had given Lyndon so much encouragement to become somebody in his own right. Said Lady Bird later, "I kept wanting to tell her, 'Don't worry, I'm not trying to run off with this young man.'"

Then it was Lady Bird's turn to take Lyndon home to meet Cap at Brick House. Lyndon was much encouraged by the impression she had made at the legendary King Ranch, the largest privately owned tract of land in the entire United States, where Representative Kleberg's mother had immediately taken to her. Lady Bird found this discerning woman to be "very much the duchess, very much the great lady." She in turn told Lady Bird that she should marry young Mr. Johnson.

Cap Taylor was much taken by Lyndon.

"Daughter," he said, "You've brought a lot of boys home. This time you've brought a man."

Lyndon was invited to stay the night and, as the pump was out of order, one of the houseboys fetched his bath water from the reservoir. That night he proposed to Lady Bird.

When she begged for time to consider his offer, her father was more specific. "Some of the best bargains are made in a hurry," he advised her.

Next morning Lyndon returned to Washington, a man very much in love, although he had known Lady Bird just one week. From the capital he sent his photograph, inscribed *For Bird, a girl of principles, ideals, and refine-*

ment, from her admirer, Lyndon. They exchanged many letters and telephone calls. Lady Bird still smiles over the trials of carrying on a courtship over a country telephone when "you hear about every third word, and so do the eavesdropping neighbors."

Seven weeks later Lyndon B. Johnson was back, begging her to marry him. She was weakening but there was still one obstacle: Aunt Effie, now sick in an Alabama hospital. It was not in Lady Bird's nature to marry without first asking the opinion of the woman who had sacrificed the best years of her own life to raise her. Even Lyndon couldn't stop her from going.

Aunt Effie was reluctant to see Lady Bird marry any young man upon whom she had not first set her seal of approval. A somewhat perplexed Lady Bird returned to Brick House, where her father said, "Go ahead"; Aunt Effie would never agree.

From there on Lyndon can take up the story: "We drove to San Antonio, and Bird still hadn't said yes until we got there. I sent a friend over to buy a ring, and we were married at the Episcopal church on the square."

Gene Boehringer was flabbergasted when Lady Bird 'phoned to say, "Lyndon and I committed matrimony last night!"

7

Long Road to Motherhood

∗ ∗

"HE crowded enough into that courtship to last us all our days, and it all came true."

Lady Bird settled with ease into her new life as the wife of a Congressman's secretary. Her early training with figures now underwent its first test, for Lyndon's salary only amounted to $267 a month.

The one-bedroom apartment they rented was a far cry from the elegance of Brick House. Lyndon's lunches, his evening tuition at George Washington University's law school, and the payments on his car devoured $100 of his earnings. Lady Bird managed the rest so cleverly that out of it she purchased an $18.17 government bond.

Aunt Effie, now reconciled to having a married niece instead of a single one, came to spend a vacation. Lady Bird was hard pressed to find sleeping accommodations for her aunt, as they were putting up a secretary and Lyndon's Uncle George Johnson at the same time.

At school Lady Bird had learned everything but how to cook. She had never been required to preside over her father's house, either. Immediately she bought her first cookbook, studied it, then decided that the secret of being simultaneously a good cook and a good hostess was to have everything ready for service at once. By preparing food in advance she could be on hand to enjoy the company of her guests instead of being in the kitchen.

Congressman and Mrs. Maury Maverick of Texas, long-time friends of Lyndon, were her first dinner guests. She served them liberal helpings of baked ham and lemon pie. Both survived to tell the tale.

With the exception of the scrubbing, which she left to a once-weekly cleaning woman, Lady Bird did her own housework, for she was determined to cut expenses.

Lyndon was ambitious, and Lady Bird was the right woman to nurture and encourage such aspirations. From the beginning he relied upon her common sense, expecting her to be at hand when needed to give him all her devotion. Their relationship has a parallel in the busy public life and private relationship of the late Sir Winston Churchill and his wife Clementine. Lyndon's first words on coming home were "Where's Bird?"; Sir Winston's were "Where's Clemmy?"

From those early Washington days, Lady Bird's entire being was dominated by her love for the human dynamo she had married. Being the wife of Lyndon B. Johnson was—and still is—for her the most important thing in the world. This has puzzled the cynical and sophisticated, who view the state of holy matrimony as something other than made in heaven. Lady Bird had been well schooled by Southern-bred Aunt Effie that one's husband is head of the family. What Lyndon wants, Lady Bird gets.

Nine months from their wedding day, Lyndon, vitally interested in Roosevelt's New Deal plans, decided to relinquish his job as a Congressman's secretary to work as Texas State Administrator of the National Youth Administration. This necessitated moving back to their beloved Texas, where they were stationed in Lady Bird's favorite Austin.

For eighteen happy, hectic months Lyndon put all his driving energy into this new occupation—getting the youngsters back to school, with part-time jobs to help support them, and teaching skills to others for specialized work.

The Johnsons' modest home was Mecca for fellow workers of the National Youth Administration and young folk hunting for jobs. Lady Bird, like Jefferson's daughter Martha Randolph at Monticello, never knew how many she would feed or entertain. She was still doing her own housework, while her cooking had improved one hundred per cent.

Deciding that Lyndon did not have enough time for reading, she first went through the books and magazine articles she though he should read, marking passages meriting his special attention.

This rewarding period of their lives ended when Texas's Tenth Congressional seat became vacant by the death of elderly Congressman James Buchanan. When Lyndon decided to try for the seat, Lady Bird believed that "the seed of running for elective office" had lurked somewhere in his subconscious since childhood. He had often heard of the prophesy made August 27, 1908, by his grandfather: "A United States Senator has been born today." That "Senator" was Lyndon.

Lyndon B. Johnson's chance to run was made possible by the woman who believed in him. First she consulted with State Senator Alvin Wirtz, a man whose word she trusted. He advised her that Lyndon's campaign would cost $10,000, but—and this was most important—only four or five of the other men running against him would have better chances.

Home she went and telephoned Cap Tom. . . .

"Daddy," she said, "do you suppose you could put ten thousand dollars in the bank for me? Lyndon wants to run for Congress."

Her father's reply was classic. "Well, today's Sunday. I don't think I could do it before tomorrow morning about nine o'clock."

Although sure that she would eventually receive the money from her mother's estate, Lady Bird saw that it was repaid $500 a month.

With an all-out Roosevelt New Deal program, Lyndon campaigned like a one-man Armada. Lady Bird regrets to this day that she couldn't actively campaign for her husband but in those days (1937) she says, "It simply wasn't done in Texas."

Lyndon won and nobody was more delighted than President Franklin D. Roosevelt, who from that day on gave the young Texas Congressman his special blessing. First invited aboard the Presidential train at Galveston, Lyndon was later given an appointment to serve on the House Naval Affairs Committee. He often breakfasted at the White House, exchanging favorite Navy talk with the President. In 1938 and 1940 he won re-election. Lyndon B. Johnson was on his way. . . .

Her husband's success did not go to Lady Bird's head. She remained the same frugal young woman who had first come to Washington as a bride. As for what she wore, she had this to say: "I like clothes. I like them pretty. But I want them to serve me, not for me to serve them—to have an important, but not a consuming part of my life."

In spite of the new $10,000 Congressman's salary, Lady Bird's friend, now Eugenia Lasseter, declared: "She was still tacky, so I told her to turn herself over to a department store and let them dress her. Bird has credited me with teaching her how to dress. But it was the store."

Neither was success constant. In 1941, Senator Morris

Sheppard of Texas died in office, and President Roosevelt persuaded young Representative Johnson to run for the vacant seat. Several others declared themselves, then dropped by the way, until only Governor W. Lee O'Daniel remained to run against Lyndon. It was a vigorous contest and, not to be outdone by the governor's hillbilly band, Lyndon campaigned with a genial singer affectionately dubbed the "Kate Smith of the South."

Although Lyndon was at first declared the winner, his opponent was in fact the new Senator with a majority of 1,311 votes. Telegrams of congratulation were still reaching Lyndon when the winning margin was announced. He took his disappointment well.

Of this early defeat Lady Bird said, "I think the experience was good for him. I can't say that a solid diet of success is good for anybody."

By this time she was used to all the excitement of a political campaign. It took its toll, especially when one lost. Lyndon was down for the moment, but his chance for a senatorship would be repeated later.

In the meantime America was keeping a wary eye on the course of World War II. Congressman Johnson had already stated that, if at any time he had to vote for his own country's entry into the conflict, he would himself take an active role. For some time he had been a member of the Naval Reserve, and when the Japanese attacked Pearl Harbor on December 7, 1941, Lyndon was the first member of the House to report for active duty. He was commissioned as a lieutenant commander and refused his annual Congressional salary of $10,000, preferring to take only his $3,000 naval pay.

Lady Bird did not return to Texas. Still childless after seven years of marriage, she though she might be most useful "sitting in" for Lyndon while he was away.

He had only been gone a day when Lady Bird arrived at his office to work without remuneration. She believed that, next to the man himself, it was his wife who cared most about his work. Lady Bird wished to reassure Lyndon's constituents that one of the Johnson team was still on the job! Not only was this practical political experience invaluable to Lady Bird Johnson, it also broadened her knowledge of Lyndon's responsibilities to the people of Texas.

Like many others, Lyndon B. Johnson found his initial days in the Navy disappointing, for instead of immediately being sent overseas he was assigned to an office in San Francisco where he was soon complaining to his brother, Sam Houston Johnson, then employed by a war agency in Denver, Colorado: "I'm not doing anything. I would be worth more to the country in Congress than I am in this assignment. I'm going to Washington and talk to the Boss [President Roosevelt]. He's got to get something done about me."

The President was sympathetic. Lyndon was assigned to the Pacific, where he worked with General Douglas MacArthur in preparing a special report for "the Boss."

There was plenty of excitement. Upon one occasion when Lyndon was aboard a Flying Fortress, christened the *Swoose*, it was forced to make an emergency landing. As it was near dusk the pilot was eager to land while there was still some light. In the midst of some desolate Australian countryside they were surprised to spot some white buildings which they knew would mean help if the plane cracked up. They were lucky, for the *Swoose* landed safely. A crew member says: "We got out. Pretty soon ranchers began coming out of nowhere, and right away Commander Johnson got busy. He began to get acquainted. They told him where we were, and some of them went off to get a truck to take us into town where we could telephone. More kept coming. Johnson was shaking hands all around. He came back and told us these were real folks—the best folks in the world, except maybe the folks in his own Texas.

"Pretty soon he knew all their first names, and they were telling him why there ought to be a high tariff on wool. There's no question—he swung that country for Johnson before we left. He was in his element. I know he sure swung the *Swoose* crew; he could carry that 'precinct' any day."

On another occasion the bomber in which Lyndon was flying had one engine destroyed by attacking Japanese fighters. He had volunteered to go along so that he might obtain for his report to President Roosevelt first-hand knowledge of actual combat conditions over New Guinea. When the bomber was attacked, Lyndon continued making notes. General MacArthur heard of his courage, and decorated him personally with the Silver Star.

With it came the citation from the General, affirming that in the face of enemy fire Commander Johnson "evidenced marked coolness in spite of the hazards involved" and that "his gallant action enabled him to obtain and return with valuable information."

While Lyndon was winning the Silver Star, Lady Bird was keeping up the distaff end, comforting the people they represented when the war took a son, reassuring mothers whose boys were wounded. Constituents back in Austin came to respect Mrs. Lyndon B. Johnson's determined efforts upon their behalf.

Among Lady Bird's extra activites was the part she played in a hilarious homemade silent movie with some friends while Lyndon was overseas. Called "Heaven Will Protect the Working Girl," Lady Bird portrayed Petunia, the working girl Heaven was protecting.

In the arm-waving melodrama, reminiscent of early Mack Sennett comedies, Lady Bird proved that she not only had a good sense of humor but a high sense of drama as well. J.B. Brumbelow as the stock mustachioed villain of the piece was no match for virtuous Petunia in her 1910 wardrobe, or her equally determined mother, played by Mary Rather, then working in Congressman Johnson's office.

When the President barred national legislators from serving in the Armed Forces, Lyndon and Lady Bird were closer than ever. Lyndon returned home to find his wife more than fascinated with politics. He was so impressed by good reports concerning her efforts in his absence that he declared, "The Tenth District would happily have elected her over me, if she had run."

Afterward Lady Bird would call this time she took over for Lyndon "the Year of Decision." She had even rented their apartment furnished to save money, taking another outside the city with Nellie Connally, whose husband would one day be Governor of Texas.

Lady Bird had emerged a politician in her own right.

Recently Lindy Boggs, Mrs. Johnson's friend, said; "Bird would be only half alive if she divorced herself from politics." This is true, for politics mean Lyndon . . . and Lyndon is her life. One must never forget that she was born a Southerner, and in the tradition of old planation families the husband heads the household; everything revolves around him.

"I was once called upon to introduce my husband at a dinner," Lady Bird has said, in attempting to explain that "something a wife feels apart from devotion."

"I said that he was an exciting man to live with; an exhausting man to keep up with . . . and most importantly, a man from whom I've learned that putting all the brains and heart and skill you have into trying to make your government work a little bit better can make a wonderful life for a man and his wife."

Several years after their marriage Lyndon could match such personal analyzing by confessing: "She [Lady Bird] is still the most enjoyable woman I've ever met. As a sweetheart, a swimmer, a rider, and a conversationalist, she is the most interesting woman I know."

After five years of living, divided between Washington and Austin, as Congressman and wife—and in ten different apartments—Lady Bird's one secret desire was a dream house. Aunt Effie and Lyndon's mother, Rebekah, often visited at the same time, and Lady Bird longed for more room and a place of her own.

Aunt Effie was very understanding and insisted upon paying most of the down payment, writing in her will that it was an advance of what she planned to leave the niece she thought of as her own daughter.

With her usual thoroughness, Lady Bird hunted for her dream house and eventually found it in the northwest section of Washington. Standing on a quiet street, the two-story brick colonial-style home seemed to be waiting for them. A screened veranda, just right for a warm night, was built in the rear. She could not wait to tell Lyndon about it.

Of course she found her husband busy talking politics to his administrative assistant, John Connally, in a conversation which he interrupted just long enough to hear the glowing details of her discovery. Then, without so much as a word, Lyndon continued his discussion. The result was one of the two occasions upon which he had ever seen Lady Bird lose her temper.

"I want that house!" Lady Bird declared. "Every woman wants a home of her own, and all that I have to look forward to is the next election!" She then left the room.

Lyndon was completely nonplused at the startling behavior of his ever-accomodating wife. Connally remarked that if it was his problem he'd buy the house. Lyndon agreed, but only after he had negotiated and knocked $2,000 off the price.

Now all that Lady Bird longed for to complete her happiness was a baby. Of these times Lyndon said recently: "Bird waited ten years to have a baby, and has lost four children through miscarriages. She is never a person who will admit her own pain. I remember one time she was running a high temperature, but she insisted that it was all right for me to go to the office. The minute that I left the room she called the doctor. She was bleeding, and in terrific pain with a tubular pregnancy, but she just won't admit pain, or ask for mercy. If she has any fault, this is it."

Lady Bird's own mother having died from the effects of a miscarriage, this courageous determination to have children showed the full strength of her character.

Now they had an eight-room house on a tree-lined street. Years later, as the wife of the President, Lady Bird would be televised there to tell, with a glow in her voice, that in front of this house her children first learned to ride their tricycles.

After the rush of his day in the city, Lyndon felt calm and refreshed by the time he reached home. It was almost like living in the country.

Lyndon B. Johnson, who has said, "Our minds acknowledge the great debt mankind owes to mothers," was always happy when his own came to stay, a sentiment that was shared equally by his wife. Lady Bird and Rebekah Johnson enjoyed a unique daughter and mother-in-law association.

"I *liked* her so very much," said Lady Bird, "and at times, you know, that is more satisfying than loving. I *enjoyed* her."

For one thing, to Lady Bird, who is a "doer," matching words with actions, Rebekah's distinguishing characteristic of never letting go once she had set her mind to achieving some worthy object was particularly appealing. Lyndon called it "stickability."

The hard times she had known as a Texas farmer's wife had not embittered her. As Lady Bird said: "She had to fight poverty, inadequate schools, and any number of things. Some people, faced with hard times, find the want of material wealth an abrasive thing and fight it. She did not; she accepted it with grace and without bitterness. If she could not have the piece of furniture she wanted, for instance, she took another and, with grace, made it her own."

After Lyndon's father died in 1937, Lady Bird found a house for Rebekah in Austin where she often visited her. Whenever Lady Bird found herself with an extra hour to spare while waiting to board a plane or train for Washington, it was always to Rebekah that she went, where they would discuss the family, favorite books, and home decorating.

"We just had the good fortune to be friends," said her daughter-in-law.

Rebekah liked to fuss over Lady Bird when she really came to stay, knowing how hard she worked in Washington. She would make Lady Bird have breakfast in bed and took a great pride in cooking the younger woman's favorite foods, including what Lady Bird called "the best spoon bread in the world."

Best of all Lady Bird remembered the thin china cups in which Rebekah loved to serve tea, for "she made a ritual of little things."

Rebekah now had time to indulge herself in her girlhood interest of collecting American pressed glass and in rereading those same books that were lifelong companions. Around her were much-loved pieces of furniture that had been her mother's, and with the old she mixed something of the new—a television set, upon the screen of which she sometimes caught glimpses of Lyndon as his star rose in Washington.

Determined to leave a record of their forebears for her children, when Rebekah visited Lyndon and Lady Bird she was all prepared to go "kinship hunting" in Maryland and Virginia. She had raised Lyndon with their stories—the Baines, Buntons, and Johnsons who had left the states of Georgia, Alabama, and Kentucky for new homes on the banks of the Pedernales River in Texas.

There was the Baptist minister, George Washington Bains (the spelling was later changed), who migrated to Texas before the War between the States, and the beautiful magnolia-skinned Eliza Bunton, "a woman queenly in carriage, of great refinement and strong family pride," who married Lyndon's grandfather, Sam Ealy, Sr. Sam, who fought the Indians at the Battle of Deer Creek, was well matched by his raven-haired wife, who "took to frontier life like the heroine she was" and who emerged from her hiding place under the floor during an Indian raid to care for the wounded. Their son, Sam Ealy, Jr., known as Little Sam although he was six feet tall, was first elected to the State Legislature in 1904, serving for nearly twelve years. Of national importance was his authorship of the Alamo Purchase Bill. Another of Lyndon's ancestors had fought against the Mexicans with a squirrel rifle in 1836 and signed the Texas Declaration of Independence.

After getting Lyndon off to work—and, later, the children to school—for fifteen years Lady Bird and her mother-in-law might set off to search out family history in some county courthouse to which the senior Mrs. Johnson had usually written beforehand.

Prior to commencing their task they would first look for a suitable place to lunch and see what antique shops there were, having Rebekah's pressed glass collection in mind.

Then it was inside the courthouse and to work among the big record books that had data of marriages, wills, deeds, and land grants. Sometimes their once or twice-weekly excursions into the past meant visiting old graveyards for the purpose of checking epitaphs, dates, spellings and names of some remote ancestors. Rebekah enjoyed picking epitaphs . . . and for her husband had chosen:

> Of purest gold from
> the Master's hand,
> A man who loved
> his fellow man.

Lady Bird could never discover whether her mother-in-law had quoted or actually written the lines herself.

At last, with much satisfaction, Rebekah traced her husband's family back to the time of the American Revolution when to her chagrin—and Lyndon's—they found this all-important ancestor to be nothing more than plain John Johnson. The rest of the family were much amused.

When, during World War II, gasoline rationing put an end to their sleuthing, they worked away at the D.A.R. Library and the Library of Congress.

Rebekah, the family historian, presented a record of her findings to Lyndon as a Christmas gift in 1954. It was published in 1965 as *A Family Album*.

One of the most pleasing aspects of Rebekah's visits to Washington was the deep friendship she made with Lady Bird's Aunt Effie, for their vacations usually coincided. Both elderly ladies enjoyed taking rides in the park, liberally quoting from their favorite poet, Robert Browning. All this was a great delight to Lady Bird, who warmly recalls that Rebekah and Aunt Effie "were crazy about each other, really devoted to each other." They usually stayed for a month, Aunt Effie having become almost as fond of Lyndon as was his mother.

At last, on March 19, 1944, after ten years of marriage and several miscarriages, Lady Bird became the mother of a brown-eyed baby girl whom Lyndon called Lynda Bird after both of them. He was so proud that night that he woke up every member of his Congressional staff to tell them the glad news.

As Lynda Bird grew into a toddler, her grandmother Rebekah could see Lyndon in the child's indomitable will, affection, and kindly sympathy for others. She also saw many traits inherited from Lady Bird, whom she noted in her family album as being a "wonderful mother."

Aunt Effie, if only for a little while, was to see and enjoy this great-niece too. When Lynda Bird was two years old Aunt Effie become very ill and had to go into a Birmingham sanatorium. Lady Bird spent several weeks with her, reading aloud favorite passages from their beloved books and talking over the past. The trees, the flowers—in fact, all beautiful things—she had first seen through this gentle woman's eyes. Who could then know that one day the entire nation would be the beneficiary in what would familiarly be called "Lady Bird's beautification project?"

There were other kinsfolk visiting the hospital, and they would lunch with Lady Bird and speak of old times. "It was a mixture of sadness, reminiscences, and sweetness," recalled Lady Bird, who was herself feeling far from well.

When Aunt Effie showed improvement, her niece returned to Washington, where she received confirmation of what she suspected to be the matter: she was pregnant again. Then came sorrow mixed with the gladness, for when a liver ailment complicated Aunt Effie's illness, the doctors forbade Lady Bird to make the long journey back to Birmingham because of the serious tubular pregnancy she had suffered only the year before. She was brokenhearted when Aunt Effie died in January 1947, and she could not be with her at the last.

(To everyone's surprise, Aunt Effie remembered to leave Rebekah Johnson a small legacy. Rebekah was delighted. She had always wanted a new pink carpet for her bedroom and now she could have one, for as Lady Bird said, "She always treated gifts as gifts and never hoarded them.")

"Joy came in the morning" when, on July 2, another daughter was born to Lady Bird. She was duly named Lucy Baines; in years to come she would change the spelling to Luci.

Rebekah's careful analysis of this new grandchild included the Baines characteristics of "self-sufficiency, poise, reserve, inner resourcefulness, and independence."

Lyndon was more practical in his summing up of their now-completed family, "It's cheaper this way, because we can all use the same luggage."

Each one of them was an LBJ!

8

The Business Woman

* *

"SHE can pick up a balance sheet and look at it with the same discernment another woman displays toward a piece of cloth," said a lawyer who handled some of Lady Bird's business affairs. And a former associate declared: "She can read a balance sheet as well as a truck driver can read a road map."

Lady Bird was to reap a rich reward from the sound foundations of her business education instilled by her father and her Uncle Claude. They trained her, early in life, to handle her own bank account—excellent experience which she would pass on to her daughters.

Toward the end of 1942, Lady Bird had heard that an Austin radio station was on the market. The Johnsons had long dreamed of owning a small-town newspaper but, as these were rising in value, could not afford one. As a substitute Lady Bird thought of radio.

"She wanted some insurance for her children's education, knowing the uncertain nature of politics, and feeling that their own future lives would be spent in politics," explained an assistant.

Besides, both Lyndon and Lady Bird had always been

interested in news media. She had majored in journalism; he had been editor of his college newspaper.

Remarried, Cap Taylor desired to pay Lady Bird the rest of her mother's inheritance which for years he had carefully invested. She also received thousands of acres of rundown Alabama cotton land, which, wisely, had been replanted with pine seedlings. After World War II began, their value increased as a source of timber, pine tar, and turpentine.

The actual cash owing from her mother's estate, of which her share was valued at $67,000, was $21,000. This she shrewdly gambled upon buying radio station KTBC and its many obligations: it owed money to practically every bank in town, had no nighttime franchise or network affiliation, possessed a frequency of a mere 250 watts, and employed nine persons. When in February 1943 the Federal Communications Commission actually approved the sale, Lady Bird was off to Austin to put KTBC's house in order.

The first thing she did was to get soap and a bucket of water and go to work cleaning the place up.

For five weeks she worked day and night, reading every contract and evaluating the staff. After seven months the station showed a profit of $18, and Lady Bird returned victoriously to Washington—and Lyndon. KTBC—to be renamed the Texas Broadcasting Corporation and later the LBJ Company—was now out of the red, and it made money ever after. Lady Bird became chairman of the board, owning 52.8 per cent of the stock and administering a further 30.9 per cent upon behalf of her daughters. Key executives were allowed to purchase the remaining shares, while Lady Bird also arranged a special employees' profit-sharing plan.

She got a C.B.S. network affiliation, which no one apparently had thought of asking for before; she added an

FM outlet and increased the power of the AM radio station from 250 to 5,000 watts.

When television was still in its infancy, and there weren't many receivers in the homes around Austin, she won an uncontested TV license on Channel 7 from the Federal Communications Commission (F.C.C.) on November 27, 1952. The TV station lost money at first, but since then it has turned into a gold mine and has become the major source of the new wealth of the First Family.

An application for renewal of the KTBC license filed with the F.C.C. showed the LBJ company, at the close of business February 28, 1962, had assets totalling $3,992,902.39, with surplus and reserves of $2,666,-533.01 and liabilities of $1,207,369.38.

In addition to stations KTBC-AM, -FM, and TV in Austin, the company was a 29 per cent stockholder in KWTX Broadcasting Company of Waco, Texas, and owned Music for Business which holds the Muzak franchise in the Austin area. KWTX Broadcasting, in turn, has various financial interests in radio and TV stations in Bryan, Texoma, and Victoria, Texas, and Ardmore, Oklahoma.

Associates claimed that Mrs. Johnson has always been the majority stockholder, chief corporation officer, and guiding genius in the LBJ Company. "She really ran that outfit," one said.

While Johnson was Vice President she operated it from a second-floor bedroom of their home, which she had converted into an office for handling the family's financial affairs.

By the time that Lyndon attained the Presidency, Lady Bird's once run-down radio station was a million-dollar enterprise, with Haskins and Sells estimating her own net worth at $2,126,198, Lynda Bird's at $490,141, and Luci Baines, $489,578!

As children, Lynda Bird and Luci were always intrigued by their mother's radio operations. Before she was old enough to attend school, it was Luci's self-appointed task to watch for the big special-delivery envelope that arrived every Sunday from Austin. Feeling very important as she marched upstairs, she would announce, "This is Mother's business."

Mixing a radio corporation in Austin with motherhood in Washington was complicated, especially when Lady Bird was called to Texas for an important meeting or emergency. While away from home on one such occasion, Lynda Bird contracted impetigo. Says her mother: "I simply could not come back because matters were crucial, but Lyndon! You would have thought that Lynda Bird had cancer, the way Lyndon behaved! He called Mrs. Albert Thomas, who got the doctor and came over and helped out. Lyndon since then has considered himself and Lera Thomas veritable lifesavers, because that skin eruption didn't finish her."

"I don't see how Lady Bird can do all the things she does without ever stubbing her toe," Lyndon once admitted. "I'll just never know, because I sure stub mine sometimes."

He was talking of her abilities as wife, businesswoman, and mother. When in 1948 he decided to have another try for the Senate, Lady Bird was right on hand to help him.

With some effort she managed to forget her own shyness before taking off on a solo campaign tour of Texas. Governor Coke Stevenson, after thirty years of political life and no defeats, was a tough opponent.

Lady Bird's task was to organize the women. In those days she hated to fly because it always made her sick, but as Lyndon told it later, "She got busy and flew all over the state."

From the start it was an exciting race, for although Governor Stevenson led in the primary he did not have the required majority of votes. A runoff was ordered between the Governor and Lyndon, who had polled the second largest number but was still 100,000 votes behind his opponent.

Many thought Lyndon's second chance in the runoff hopeless, "But," said Lady Bird, "at least I wanted to narrow that margin, not only for Lyndon but for the sake of those folks who had shoveled so much love and sweat and time and money into the campaign."

First with the aid of a good friend, Mrs. Max Brooks, she listed all the clubwomen they knew in Texas, in addition to contacting acquaintances from National Youth Administration, school, and college days.

She traveled into the highways and byways of Texas, wooing the voters. No women's gathering was too little for her friendly "Howdy"; no home too poor. Wherever she went, scores of small-town folks turned out to greet and shake her hand. This was no time to fear speechmaking, or to be shy of praising Lyndon, which she still found embarrassing. Knowing that she had to "sell" him to her audience, she did it simply by deciding, "These people are just like me, so I have no reason to be scared."

On the night before the election, the car she was riding in careened off the road, then flipped over twice in the mud. Said Lady Bird, "All I could think of as we were turning over was that I sure wished I'd voted absentee."

Getting up, she hitched a ride, reached her destination, borrowed a dress from her hostess, and shook hands with two hundred women. Then she joined Lyndon in San Antonio to make a speech. "She didn't even tell me about that accident," he said, "for fear it'd worry me."

About midnight, when she was changing her dress, getting ready to press on for Austin where she wanted to do some last-minute campaigning, he saw some of her bruises and demanded to know the truth.

"But she went right on to Austin and got on the telephone with Mother and my sisters, and they called everyone in the Austin phone book on my behalf. We carried Austin three to one, thanks to that, but we barely carried the state by eighty-seven votes."

However, because of the small margin there were still many legal battles to win between August and January. Lady Bird recalls those long months of uncertainty, likening them to "the feeling that presses in on a person in a wartime concentration camp under prolonged questioning."

Finally, "Landslide Lyndon," as other Senators dubbed him, was sworn in.

With Lyndon's future settled for the next six years, Lady Bird decided to indulge herself by redecorating their new house. Lyndon insisted upon "helping" with his advice, which might have been a minor catastrophe if she had not diplomatically chosen three samples of any fabric or furnishing she could live with before letting Lyndon make a "safe" selection. It worked . . . and she painted their bedroom yellow "because Lyndon thinks it's such a cheerful color for starting the day."

Working sometimes eighteen hours a day, Lyndon Baines Johnson seemed even then to be destined for great places. The late Sam Rayburn, his father's great friend and Lyndon's own trusted mentor, who was then Speaker of the House, was most helpful. Lyndon was selected to serve on the Armed Services Committee, where he performed a monumental task.

At the beginning of 1950 he called for a reassessment of the foreign and military policy of the United States. He introduced the resolution that a Preparedness Investigating Subcommittee of the Senate Armed Services Committee should be established. It was passed, and Lyndon B. Johnson, the freshman Senator, became the new committee's chairman.

Lady Bird was proud indeed. . . .

On Tuesdays she attended the Senate Ladies' Red Cross unit, for war had broken out in Korea. Among the women wrapping bandages was another devoted wife, Patricia Nixon, whose husband was Vice President Richard Nixon.

Lady Bird admired the perfectionist Mrs. Nixon, who often with little advance notice had been called upon by First Lady Mamie Eisenhower to perform the exciting task of White House hostess. Pat had gone a long way since her student days, when by necessity she had been obliged to work her way through college. Now, like Lady Bird, she was raising two daughters and proving an asset to her husband's political ambitions as well.

With her ever-growing list of appointments, Pat Nixon had reluctantly relinquished the task of doing her own housework. When her husband was first elected Vice President she did not let the importance of his new position go to her head and rush right out to engage a maid. For four years she continued to do the cooking and to vacuum the floors like any other American housewife. In those days a morning caller might be whisked into her kitchen for coffee while she prepared the children's lunch.

From practical experience, Lady Bird Johnson could appreciate a woman like that.

"It's the job that's important, not you and me," Lady Bird had more than once told her daughters. "Naturally they crave more of our companionship and attention, but I have tried to impress on them that their father's job is important. I assure them, however, that such importance doesn't rub off on them."

Lady Bird was never happy at having to leave her youngsters so much because of Lyndon's senatorial duties. She was hurt when they called themselves "deprivileged" children. When saying goodbye, recalling her own motherless childhood, she would whisper in their ear; "Remember, you are loved."

Her business obligations in Texas and Alabama, in addition to the receptions and parties they were obliged to attend as new members of official Washington society, meant less time with Lynda Bird and Luci Baines.

"That has been one of the costs," Lady Bird said years later. "It is one of the bills you have to pay for the job your husband has." Nevertheless, the ties between parents and daughters have always been very close.

Fortunately, from the time that Luci was two, Lady Bird had Helen Williams to organize the household and take charge of the girls when she had to be away. Mary Rather and Willie Day Taylor, members of Lyndon's staff, often helped with the children. Mary saw Lynda Bird through the mumps and was the recipient of the first cherry pie the child ever baked: Lynda Bird tripped with the sticky offering, which landed in Mary's lap! Actually Luci was the domestic member of the family. She would fly for a mop when something was dropped on the carpet. And her cookies were edible.

Both little girls had inherited their father's outgoing friendliness and were far from shy. From an early age they were allowed to greet dinner guests and chat for a little while. The late Sam Rayburn, an elderly bachelor, adored them both. They told him their childhood secrets, and he loved to attend their birthday parties.

Early in their lives Lady Bird taught them the value of self-confidence and independence.

Christmas was always the favorite time in the Johnson household. They would be home in Texas, for Christmas Eve could never be spent any place but at Grandmother's house; Rebekah Johnson liked to have her children and grandchildren about her on that most wonderful of nights. Lady Bird recalls how they all loved going; how large the tree was and how "well gifted." The children would plunder the tree; the floor would be covered with colored wrappings. Then Rebekah served homemade fruitcake. Each year the seasonal ritual was the same. Said Lady Bird, "It never varied."

Once Lynda Bird arranged her own nativity play in the way that children will. Her mother walked in and asked what they were doing. Seriously Lynda Bird explained that they were "playing Jesus."

Somewhat nonplused, Lady Bird asked her daughter to explain herself, whereupon Lynda Bird said that one seven-year-old friend was playing Mary, another Joseph, while Luci was the Baby Jesus.

Curious, Lady Bird wanted to know which part was Lynda Bird's.

"I'm Roy Rogers, of course," she answered.

At about this time, when Luci was three, a very important addition was made to the household in the form of a very determined beagle puppy. Lady Bird has told the story best in these words:

"Our Luci Baines, when she was three years old, began to ask for a dog. I had any number of reasons for not wanting one. In the first place, after years of yearning for them, I had just acquired some beautiful carpets of which I was very proud; and second, we were moving back and forth between Washington and Austin each year. I had had the experience of traveling with a cat, and I didn't want to repeat it with a dog, so I just sorta delayed.

"I didn't know how to go about finding a dog," she continued. "I couldn't find the right kind of dog. You know—all the reasons you think of for not doing the things you don't want to do. Then one night, when a blizzard was raging outside, Lyndon came home with a big smile, a heavy overcoat, and a big box in his arms. He put the box down on the living-room rug and called Luci Baines to come and look.

"Luci got down and peered into the box, and when she

raised her face, I have never seen such a beatific expression on any angel. In the box was a beagle, age six weeks, and as cute and lively as he could be. He came to be the joy of the whole family, but he was more especially Luci Baines' dog, except for the period when Lyndon had his heart attack, and then he devoted himself entirely to Lyndon."

Lyndon had journeyed in a blizzard down to a kennel near Middleburg, Virginia. . . . The dog was duly named Little Beagle Johnson so that his initials would match their own LBJ.

Luci laughs even now at her mother's reaction to Little Beagle's unexpected arrival:

"Oh, my rugs!"

9

Their Hearts' True Home

* *

DURING the latter part of the last century, Richard Jefferies, the essayist, wrote of an old gabled house in Buckhurst Park, England, words that might equally be applied to the LBJ ranch house: "Their rooms they liked of many shapes, and not at right angles in the corners, nor all on the same dead level of flooring. You had to go up a step into one, and down a step into another, and along a winding passage into a third, so that each part of the house had its individuality. To these houses life fitted itself and grew to them; they were not mere walls, but became part of existence. A man's house was not only his castle, a man's house was himself. He could not tear himself away from his house, it was like tearing up the shrieking mandrake by the root, almost death itself."

Lyndon had always loved the old house which he had known from childhood. It was no great architectural triumph, having been built first for safety and durability and then added to for livableness. The original old stone ranch house was a grim reminder of the days of Indian raids; the later wooden additions had been made in happier, safer times to accommodate an ever-growing family.

Lyndon's aunt, Mrs. Clarence Martin, had lived in the house for fifty years when the Johnsons bought it in 1951. They had been visiting friends in their home state, and Lyndon had one more ranch house that he wanted to show Lady Bird. In those days there was no bridge to cross when visiting the run-down old house, so much less luxurious than the others they had visited that weekend. Yet that little stone ranch house was destined to become the most famous in Texas: the Little White House.

"Let's buy it!" said Lyndon with his usual enthusiasm.

Lady Bird had only just achieved her dream house in Washington. Now she was frankly appalled at the work to be done on Lyndon's new enterprise. "I could hardly bear the thought of it!" was her immediate reaction.

As usual she subjugated her own wishes to her husband's, the result being the LBJ Ranch as we know it today. Years later Lady Bird wrote, "For me it means continuity, permanence, and roots."

The house faced the Pedernales River which flows leisurely through green pastures. Lynda Bird and Luci grew up thinking of this house as their only real home. "Like it?" exclaimed Lynda Bird, replying to a question. "That's like asking whether a cow likes her calf!"

Located in the Texas hill country some sixty miles north of San Antonio where Lyndon was born and went to school, the terrain is both gentle and harsh, as its mood may be. There are 415 acres set in a land of rocks and hills which once tested the endurance of Lyndon's forebears. The cedars and live oaks stay green the year round; the latter shed not in fall but in spring.

The day they decided to buy the ranch, Lady Bird watched the sheep grazing down at the water's edge. It reminded her of a Biblical scene. Here men work hard and yet still find time to visit and enjoy a game of dominoes with their neighbors. It is a land of deer, wild turkey, racoons, and Angora goats . . . of Spanish oak and flaming red sumac. Lady Bird had to acquire a feeling for their new home. "After I came to sense how completely Lyndon was immersed in the rocks and hills and live oaks of this, his own native land, and how much strength he drew from it, I gradually began to get wrapped up in it myself. I always have loved living on the land. It was just that I had grown up on such a completely different sort of land."

With her usual efficiency, Lady Bird went ahead with restoring the house that Lyndon loved. Part of it was more than a hundred years old while the surrounding live oaks were more than three hundred. These she too began to love as she took her early morning strolls along the river.

She used the colors suggested by the land itself for her decorating schemes—vivid greens, corals, browns, yellows, and blues.

Porfirio Salinas, the Mexican artist, provided some of the paintings to hang on the walls. . . . Bowls of brass and copper are usually filled with wildflowers—Indian paintbrush, black-eyed Susans, and bluebonnets. How Lady Bird loves bluebonnets! Acres of them were planted at her direction.

Most of the original furnishings came from the contents of a house that Lady Bird bought from an elderly lady in Washington. At the housewarming festivities, in addition to the usual pies and preserves, rancher neighbors arrived bearing Queen Anne's wreath to plant by the fences.

The living room, painted a pleasing orange and green, is part of the original house built by Lyndon's great-grandfather. There behind the thick stone walls lived his sturdy pioneer ancestors.

In various rooms are attractive reminders of Rebekah Baines Johnson, her marble-topped dresser being used in one of the bedrooms. Over the fireplace of the Friendship Memento room hangs the silver saddle presented to Lyndon by President López Mateos of Mexico. The enormous mahogany desk was a gift for Lyndon from his staff. It was the one he used while serving as Minority Leader.

The master bedroom boasts a mahogany double bed, rocking chair, large dresser and a closet equally divided between husband and wife.

The rooms are linked by communal piped-in music and a loudspeaker system that would amaze the pioneer ancestors, could they return.

Rebekah Johnson often visited her son and his family at the ranch, occupying a downstairs room for her convenience. There in the old house Lady Bird has preserved many memories associated with her mother-in-law, including a lilac sweetheart quilt. In 1954 Rebekah gave her son as his Christmas present the genealogical album she had made, which recently he has shared with fellow Americans, and of which Lady Bird has said: "Lyndon appreciated the book at the time and I think has grown to enjoy it more in the eleven years since she gave it to him, although he always had a rare and very well justified understanding of what a great woman his mother was."

When Rebekah died on September 12, 1958, it was fitting that she should be buried in the family cemetery on the LBJ Ranch. Over her grave her family placed the epitaph:

<blockquote>
None knew thee but to love
thee
None named thee but to
praise.
</blockquote>

Over the years Lady Bird has supervised the expansion of the main house to accommodate the growing demands of public life. A separate guesthouse for eight visitors was such a success that Vice President and Mrs. Hubert Humphrey have copied it for their vacation house in Minnesota.

However, the basic homely feeling of the old house remains. The evening air may be gay with music from guitar strings in barbecue time and with young folks' laughter, yet on the comfortable front porch those who prefer may rock gently in the evening breeze. As she once did as Aunt Effie's little girl, Lady Bird is still thrilled by each new Texas sunset, often expressing her feelings in words.

The guests are warned beforehand to attend a party "if the Lord is willin' and the creek don't rise."

"We're white-faced Hereford people," she is likely to tell a stranger, and there at hand are the proud cattle to prove it. . . . "Cattle are more profitable than sheep," Lyndon once explained to the press: "I made only two hundred dollars last year from sheep and ten to eleven thousand dollars from cattle."

When Vice President, Lyndon presented President Kennedy with a pregnant Hereford. Kennedy quipped, "Send it to Walton. [William Walton was a former Georgetown neighbor.] He'll know what to do with it."

Lyndon was not happy with such a suggestion. "What's Walton's phone number?" he demanded. "I want to make damn sure he's there when my cow arrives!"

Although today the LBJ Ranch is often put to diplomatic uses because Lyndon is proud of showing off the hospitality and friendliness of his own particular part of America, it is a serious business concern.

Dale Malachek is in charge of the development of a purebred white-faced Hereford herd. Each summer homegrown peaches are frozen by the quart, okra pickled, and vegetables canned. The freezers are filled with beef and pork; the Johnsons make their own deer sausage. Lady Bird brings her canned peaches and corn back to the White House for winter use, where during a meal she can understandably brag "that came from our own garden."

She is particularly partial to peaches, so that when President López Mateos of Mexico was due to arrive at the ranch and she was asked by the Mayor of nearby Stonewall —population 200—what he could do to help, she replied, "Do you know of anyone in town who has some pretty peaches?"

Mayor Simon Berg replied that he would see what he could find, and that same afternoon up drove a truck with a bushel of the most splendid peaches Lady Bird had ever seen. These had actually been hand-sorted from a thousand bushels of fruit picked in neighboring orchards. When the Mexican party left next day for New York, they were each carrying a sack of peaches. It is with such sincere and simple courtesies that both the LBJ Ranch and its owners have endeared themselves to visiting dignitaries from many lands.

Chancellor Ludwig Erhard of Germany found himself the guest of honor at a barbecue served in Stonewall High School's White Springs gymnasium where he ate spareribs, baked beans and potato salad, washed down with coffee served in tin cups.

Lady Bird candidly admits that "there is no nice way to eat spareribs. . . ." Her own favorite recipes include turkey dressing, pickled okra, and deer bacon.

At the high school barbecue Lyndon jovially placed a ten-gallon Texas hat on Chancellor Erhard's head before presenting some thirty other guests with the big felt souvenirs. He even creased some of the hats—a serious Texas ritual.

President Ayub Khan of Pakistan, who had once been treated to an elaborate banquet party at historic Mount Vernon by Jacqueline Kennedy so that the *New York Herald Tribune* saw fit to ask, "What would Martha have said?" was given more homely treatment when he visited the Johnsons' ranch. Whereas Jacqueline served crab meat mimosa and *couronne-de-riz-clamart* (chicken with rice) and was afterward subjected to a battery of criticism from indignant American housewives who did not approve of an all-French menu, at the LBJ, President Ayub fell in love with good home cooking. Years before at Hyde Park Eleanor Roosevelt had delighted the King and Queen of England when she served them hot dogs, "an all-American delicacy" they had never tasted before!

Lady Bird's much-loved cook, Mrs. Zephyr Wright, is accustomed, after twenty years, to preparing food for a great variety of people. Best of all she likes to cook Lyndon's favorite recipes. Zephyr's speciality is Pedernales Chili.

Perhaps the most memorable part of the Pakistani President's visit was the drive by car and jeep at dusk to a cattle guard where the wild deer loved to feed. As the headlights were dimmed, an air of expectancy and hush came over the entire group. Suddenly six graceful deer leapt over the barrier with the precision of a troupe of ballet dancers, disappearing into the tall grass. Lyndon was heard to murmur to the visiting president, "Where the deer and the antelope play." Then he explained the words of the old cowboy song to his guest.

The Johnsons' rancher neighbors are always guests at such functions—so that the visitors meet some ordinary Americans instead of only diplomats and socialites—so back at the ranch Texans and Pakistanis exchanged stories of Texan rattlesnakes and Pakistani pythons.

When President Ayub Khan returned to his own country, more than half of his press conference dealt with Texas!

As Lyndon likes to say, "This is the part of the world where people love you while you live, care when you're sick, and miss you when you're dead."

When Lady Bird is home at the ranch she is busy supervising everything. New magazines and fresh candy are a must in the guest rooms. At other times when she is in

Washington and preparations must be under way before her own arrival, she can reliably depend on trusted Texan "help." An Austin florist, R. A. Lewis, knows the dimensions and color schemes of the main ranch house rooms and, most important, Lady Bird's personal tastes, so that he can quickly create floral arrangements that will please her. When in residence it is the wildflowers that she likes to use best, her guests often picking them. Richard Seppala, the Finnish Ambassador, once joined Elizabeth Carpenter in picking bluebonnets in the pasture. Bess Abel, White House Social Secretary, was responsible for arranging them in copper bowls.

The Johnsons love to take visitors careening over the ranch in their cars, equipped with two-way radios, on which they kept up a running commentary such as:

"Where are you going now, Honey?"

"We're heading in. I've got to see how supper's coming."

"O.K. I'll take this bunch to see the cemetery."

The best way to get out to the ranch is to fly in by airplane. The Johnsons discovered this long ago, built a landing strip, turned a barn into a hangar, and kept Lady Bird's airplane there. This short landing strip will accommodate small private planes and helicopters.

For security reasons today, whenever the Johnsons return to their ranch the public is faced with a sign reading: RESTRICTED AREA—AUTHORIZED PERSONNEL ONLY. This notice is there of necessity, not choice, for the Women's National Press Club in Washington gave the doormat that proclaims, "All the world is welcome here."

Popular with their neighbors, once when the Pedernales decided to flood, ruining their best pecan trees, Lyndon and pilot Ray Goodwin went by helicopter upon a rescue mission. When one old lady refused to leave without her dog, Lyndon went back to get it. The animal bit him.

During the flood of 1952 Lady Bird was alone at the

ranch with the children. "Lady Bird was here and Luci was just a baby," said the President, recalling the incident, "and she was carrying another baby, and she lost that baby as a result of the flood."

Flying in to get his family, the single-motor airplane crashed and tore off a wing as they got ready for takeoff. Lady Bird had to be taken out on the back road by car.

To reach the LBJ Ranch one drives through Dripping Springs and Hye before coming to the Little White House sitting among its live oaks by the Pedernales River. (Pedernales means stones or rocks in Spanish.)

A long white gate opens onto the property, and then the road leads across a narrow lake made by damming the river. The neatly landscaped yard, the simple round white portals of the porch, and a Friendship Walk with one stone inscribed "John Kennedy, 1960" are endearing features.

There are a welcoming delegation of peahens and a peacock christened "Pistol Pete" by a newspaper reporter. Among the two hundred Herefords is an agreeable bull called "Friendly Nixon." The 415 acres boast plenty of small game in addition to the white-tailed deer and wild turkeys.

Lyndon's ancestors came here in the late 1840's, their first home being a stone and log cabin built impregnable as a small fort against the threat of Comanche raids. Nearby is the simple little farmhouse where on Thursday, August 27, 1908, Lyndon was born, a large baby weighing nearly ten pounds. One can almost picture his young father, Sam Ealy Johnson, galloping off on his horse Fritz to announce to his parents in the next farmhouse:

"It's a boy!"

It is a little house with a deep, sloping roof, somewhat dilapidated by wear but pioneerlike and sturdy, bespeaking all that is best in our country. In late years Lyndon's mother was embarrassed to see him proudly show official visitors the run-down structure, "where I got my start."

Then there is the one-room schoolhouse in which a future President was taught. It is all rather heartwarming and encouraging in this age of spacecraft and big business. Seeing the little school, one can believe that in America any boy can still grow up to be President!

"Every time I lifted my hand, she would be there," Lyndon said after the serious heart attack that felled him on Luci's eighth birthday, July 2, 1955.

The youngest Senate Leader in history admitted to feeling tired, which was unusual. Fresh air and rest seemed the natural remedy for a man who loved the outdoor life, so he decided to spend the Fourth of July weekend on the Virginian estate of George Brown, a fellow Texan. On the way "a closed-in" feeling overcame him, so Lyndon asked his driver, Norman Edwards, to switch on the air conditioner —but it was already in operation.

The tension increased, so that by the time he arrived at the Brown home his chest seemed to be holding "a two-hundred-pound weight."

George Brown thought that some bicarbonate of soda was needed. He noticed Lyndon's labored breathing. Another guest, Senator Clinton P. Anderson, a member of the Cardiac Club, recognized all the symptoms of a heart attack. Brown called a doctor, to whom Lyndon said, "If you think it might be a heart attack, let's act as though we know it is."

Meanwhile, at their home in Washington Lady Bird was preparing for Luci's party when she received by phone the news of her husband's illness. She left immediately for Bethesda Naval Hospital so as to be there when he arrived.

As Lyndon was lifted from the stretcher his immediate thoughts were for her. Turning to an aide he instructed:

"My money clip's in my coat pocket. Give it to Bird. She'll be needing cash right away. If things don't turn out all right, my will is in the safe at the office."

Then he looked up, and Lady Bird was there.

"Stay with me, Bird," he begged, holding her hand.

A few minutes later he went into shock.

For the next six weeks Lyndon was hospitalized, with Lady Bird staying in an adjoining room. The Senate Leader was determined that the seriousness of his condition should be approached with honesty.

"Announce it to the press," he ordered George Reedy, his press secretary. "Don't kid anybody. Don't say I'm in for a checkup. Say I had a heart attack—a belly buster."

He displayed a surprising realism toward death, so that a few days after his attack, when Lady Bird wanted to know what she should do about two suits he had on order—one brown and the other blue—feeling they might not fit him when he was well enough to need them, he managed to joke: "We might as well keep the dark blue one, Bird. We'll need that one, either way." Even Lady Bird had to smile.

Outwardly she had remained perfectly calm, although to a close friend she whispered, "When Lyndon is out of danger and the crisis is past, I just want to go off alone somewhere and cry."

They had always been close, yet now in their time of trouble Lyndon and Lady Bird Johnson seemed even more so.

"Lyndon wanted me around twenty-four hours a day," she later recalled. "He wanted me to laugh a lot and always to have lipstick on. During those days, we rediscovered the meaning and freshness of life."

Rebekah Johnson, Lyndon's mother, was a tower of strength to them both. Although seventy-four years old at the time, she took her first plane flight from Texas to Washington to be with them. She insisted that her son would recover to fulfill the great role she had never doubted history had waiting.

When on the way to the hospital, Lyndon had asked for a cigarette, the doctor replied, "Senator, you've had your last cigarette."

"Take away my seniority in the Senate," retorted the patient, "but don't take me off my three packs a day." Nevertheless he gave up smoking altogether, testing himself by keeping a pack on the table by his bed.

"Determined to get well, he even improved upon his doctor's orders. They set his new caloric intake at 1,500; he decided it should be 1,200. His weight decreased from 225 to 184 pounds. Later when he was on his feet the doctors said he should walk a mile per day. Lyndon measured half a mile on a pedometer given him by his sister, then walked this distance and back, in addition to an extra hundred yards.

By the time he was able to leave the hospital for recuperation at the ranch, the Johnsons were more united than ever. They had deepened their marriage, appearing even more close. With time on his hands, Lyndon grew to know the children better, joining them at dominoes and listening to their childhood chatter of school and friends.

"Daddy, it's so nice to have you around the house so much," decided Luci after a Sunday morning breakfast.

To a friend the convalescent senator confessed: "I've thrown away the whip. That heart attack taught me to appreciate some things a busy man sometimes almost forgets. I'm learning all over again how to live."

He still hated to have Lady Bird out of his sight. Observed Lynda Bird: "Daddy worships Mother. He tells her his problems and seeks her advice. It's just that he doesn't realize that sometimes she might want to weep on *his* shoulder."

At first after returning home from the hospital, Lyndon proved a good patient, but with returning strength he daily became more like a prisoner. It took all of Lady Bird's tact to keep him quiet yet occupied.

After first boning up on the subject herself, Lady Bird taught Zephyr Wright how to prepare low-caloried foods, measuring everything upon a new pair of scales. Dr. Willis Hurst, the heart specialist, had accompanied them to the ranch, remaining until Lyndon was safely settled. He advised that the Senator should take life quietly for some time.

Gradually the country replenished Lyndon's strength and again he took an interest in daily happenings. A swimming pool was built in the garden; an elderly relative's home redecorated a short distance from the ranch. Adlai Stevenson wrote Lady Bird: "Thanks for the reassuring note about Lyndon. I saw a comforting picture in the newspaper the other day, but I hear he shows marked signs of postponed juvenile delinquency in the sickroom. If he isn't behaving properly, let me know and I'll send a posse of assorted Democrats down there to help you out."

There was no need, for Lyndon was getting well. Relatives and neighbors would gather to talk lazily under the trees while his constant companion Little Beagle would lie stretched out asleep on his lap. A temporary office had been set up in the living room.

Six months after his heart attack Lyndon Baines Johnson was ready to resume his duties, thanks in no small measure to his wife's selfless devotion.

"Where's Bird?" had been his first words on waking during the dark days of illness . . . and always would come those soft, reassuring words, "Here I am, darling."

10

The Second Lady

* *

"LYNDON is a great hand at saying what he wants and then expecting me to implement it. He wants music in every room, so I installed it. Once he wanted a new lawn for a party in three weeks—something almost impossible to achieve in the fall—but he got it."

Now it was Lady Bird's turn to say what she wanted. Because of Lyndon's powerful position as Senate Leader, she was often asked to make speeches. Aware of her inadequacy in this field, she enrolled in a speech series arranged by Hester Provenson.

"I got real annoyed with myself for being so shy and quiet," Lady Bird explained, "and never having anything to say when asked to speak. I took the course, and it turned out to be one of the most delightful, expanding experiences I've ever had."

The speech class was a great success, although her first press conference turned into a family rather than a solo affair. It had been arranged to coincide with Lyndon's attending a National Press Club stag dinner, as Lady Bird thought she was not ready to perform in front of him. However, he slipped away during the entertainment part of the dinner, and Lady Bird had scarcely begun to answer questions when in he strode. Then twelve-year-old Luci and Little Beagle Johnson entered the picture. Lady Bird glowed. . . .

When Lyndon's name was suggested as a possible Democratic candidate in the 1960 elections, Lady Bird found herself more in the spotlight than ever. At a Democratic Women's Club affair she said: "Usually at a dinner like this, I listen to someone introduce Lyndon with words of praise and approval, all of which I underwrite with joy. But I want to introduce him in a more personal way tonight, as an exciting man to live with, an exhausting man to keep up with, a man who has worn well in the twenty-five years we've been together, and, most important, a man from whom I've learned that to put all the brains and heart and skill you have into the job of trying to make your government work a little better can be a wonderful life for a man and his wife."

Frankly, Lyndon's chances of becoming the Democratic candidate were not good, although fellow contender John F. Kennedy himself declared: "I know all the other candidates pretty well, and I frankly think I'm as able to handle the Presidency as any of them, or abler—all except Lyndon, and he hasn't got a chance."

Lyndon's Southern birth was considered by many as a detriment to his chances, although he stressed the point that his part of Texas had more in common with the Rocky Mountain and Western states than with the Southland. Ironically he was far from popular in the South because of his record on civil rights. In 1951 he had guided the Senate through its first civil rights bill since the Reconstruction days. Then he was instrumental in defeating a Southern filibusterer who was trying to impede this same cause.

Lyndon played a waiting game, not announcing his Presidential candidacy until a week before the Democratic Convention was slated to open in Los Angeles. Lady Bird was again ready to campaign.

"I find it interesting and exhilarating. . . . I learn a lot," she said. "I feel it's important for me to go along. I think people can assess a man better when they know what kind of wife and family he has. They are interested in the total man. I can be helpful to him on trips, too, by ordering breakfast in the room and making sure there's saccharine for his coffee. I try to remind him of his diet without being obnoxious. I try to draw the line at nagging. He's kind enough or flattering enough to value my judgment. I'm likely to have the same basic sort of reaction that many of his constituents would. Lyndon is quite capable of learning from and following the directions of anybody he thinks is wise and knowledgeable, and to a little extent he thinks that I am."

So, the four LBJs set out for California and the nominating convention. A recent cardiogram showed no evidence of damage from his heart attack. Lady Bird's months of loving care and emphasis on his dieting had been invaluable.

At the Los Angeles Biltmore Hotel, a crowd of supporters awaited the arrival of the Johnsons, led by the red, white, and blue ensembles denoting the lady volunteers, so much a part of every political convention, and in this instance known as "Ladies for Lyndon."

Lyndon was the first to acknowledge the cheering, then Lady Bird and Lynda Bird each went to the microphone. Luci stole the show when it came her turn. At thirteen she simply said, "Gosh, I wish I had as many boy friends as there are people in this room."

Perle Mesta, former Minister to Luxemburg and by this time an American institution, was at hand to hostess a reception for the Johnsons at the Coconut Grove. She was for Lyndon all the way.

The suspense was hard on Lynda Bird and Luci, so that when Lyndon lost out to Jack Kennedy, being placed second with 409 votes to his 761, Luci could no longer control her emotions, bursting into tears. This was Lady Bird's finest hour. Turning to the sobbing child she said very quietly, "Remember, dear, you are loved." It was the old familiar phrase she had so often impressed upon both children from babyhood. Then, outwardly calm, she took the unhappy girls back to the Biltmore where the newsmen were waiting to ask how she felt about her husband's defeat.

"I wouldn't be saying what is true if I didn't say that I'm disappointed for my country," was her reply. "Lyndon would have made a noble President . . . a tough, can-do President. But as a mother and a wife and a woman who wakes up in the morning wanting to call her day her own, I have a sizable feeling of relief."

For these observations, Mrs. Johnson received the admiration of all the newsmen . . . and newswomen. She has never lost it since.

When Lyndon accepted second place on the Presidential ticket, Lady Bird entered a new phase of frantic activity. Jacqueline Kennedy, who was pregnant, was not allowed by her doctors to attend the convention for fear the excitement might cause a miscarriage (such a thing having happened at the 1956 convention).

It was obvious that Mrs. Kennedy would be unable to play an active part in the grueling campaign ahead and that her place would largely be taken by Lady Bird, whom she had met only at large social functions. They came to know each other much better when Lyndon and Lady Bird flew to the Kennedy compound, Hyannis Port. At this time

Lady Bird, sympathetic because of her own unhappy record of miscarriages, spent her time admiring paintings that Jacqueline had done and photographs she had taken. Lady Bird, being quite a photographer herself, was interested, especially in the Washington scenes.

When Jacqueline complained that she felt "dreadful" because she was unable to do more to help her husband at this the most important period of his life and asked the older woman what she should do, Lady Bird suggested she invite the press to Hyannis Port to meet her at her own home. Jacqueline took Lady Bird's advice.

As for Lady Bird, that autumn she traveled some 35,000 miles for the Democratic cause. With Mrs. Rose Kennedy, Jack's mother, and several of the Kennedy sisters, the distaff side was well represented. "So glad y'all came," Lady Bird repeated hundreds of times to the thousands of women who shook her hand.

With quick diplomatic answers, Lady Bird was more than a match for those who sought to entangle her in some thorny issue, of which Kennedy's Roman Catholic faith was a prime example. "The more deeply one reads the Bible, and the more one thinks about it, the more fair he will be," she was quick to declare, noting too that Lyndon had "plenty of blood-kin Baptist relatives" to even the odds. This touch of humor drew the remark from a reporter that the largest Baptist college in the world, Baylor University, seemed opposed to a Catholic President. Lady Bird's feathers were unruffled.

"Lyndon's great-grandfather," she said, "was the second president of Baylor and he converted Sam Houston. We still have the letter from Sam Houston to him. It's framed and hanging on the wall. If my house was on fire, I'd grab that letter on the way out."

They called Lady Bird the Democrats' secret weapon, yet during the greater part of the campaign she was undergoing a great personal sorrow, for her father, Cap Taylor, was dying. Now eighty-six years old, he had been in and out of the hospital for a year.

Late in September, Lady Bird had to leave the campaign at Houston to fly to Marshall, Texas, where the doctors had decided to amputate her father's gangrenous leg. For twelve hours she stayed at the hospital until the immediate crisis was past, then returning to "the front."

Each night, wherever she was, she called the hospital; then, two weeks after the amputation, while campaigning in Arizona she received a call that Cap was sinking. She phoned Lyndon and her daughters, then flew back to Marshall. Lynda Bird and Luci joined her at Dallas.

Again her father bridged the crisis; again Lady Bird returned to campaign for Jack Kennedy and Lyndon. Her train stopped at many points through Tennessee . . . she spoke in Virginia and Delaware. . . . Then came another call to Marshall.

For two days she sat beside her father. On October 22 he died. She begged Lyndon not to come "until just in time for the funeral" because he "suffered" so on such occasions. Lyndon refused to listen, joining her at once. He had never forgotten how Cap had immediately approved him as his future son-in-law, now so many years ago.

At Brick House, with her friends of childhood days arriving laden with tasty pies and baked hams with which to feed the out-of-town mourners, Lady Bird exchanged stories of times gone by.

The services were held in Karnack Methodist Church, built on land which he had donated. Not far away were the Church of Christ and the Baptist Church, also built on land given by her father. The elementary and high schools were likewise erected on Taylor land. Lady Bird felt a sense of pride mingled that afternoon with her sorrow, for all around were examples of Cap's warmth and generosity.

Then, after a day spent with her brother Tony, she returned to help the Democrat cause. She had become their answer to Pat Nixon, hard-working wife of Richard M. Nixon, the Republican candidate.

In Greensboro, North Carolina, her plane left the fog-shrouded airstrip, zigzagging into a field. Fortunately it did not turn over and catch fire. The way that Lady Bird recovered from the shock and proceeded to shake the hundreds of outstretched hands made it difficult to believe that this was the same woman who had once been afraid to fly. However, she did tell the North Carolinians that she was "glad to be on firm ground again," before taking off once more in the same plane to make a speech in Fayetteville.

In New York City she was asked by a large press conference what she thought were the chances for winning the election. Her reply was grass roots and forthright:

"I can judge only what I see, and my hands and feet tell me that the prospects are awfully good."

When Lyndon developed a sore throat, making his scheduled television appearance on Dave Garroway's important *Today* program a physical impossibility, Lady Bird apologetically went in his place. She was an unprecedented success. In Georgia the Democrats declared a *Lady Bird Johnson Day*, while in Alabama her kissing cousins came out in full force to greet her aboard the LBJ Victory Special train. She refused to be drawn into the petty controversy being fought in the press over which prospective First Lady spent more on clothes—Pat Nixon or Jacqueline Kennedy.

"I guess I'm pretty unremarkable as far as clothing goes," was her simple answer. "No Paris, alas," she added with a smile.

Likewise she diplomatically refrained from a critical comment concerning Mrs. Kennedy's bouffant hairdo, which at that time had not achieved its later popularity. "I think it's more important what's inside the head than what's outside," said Lady Bird.

It was Lady Bird's natural charm that pleased the masses. No question was too unimportant. A reporter once wanted to know how ever she managed to cope with a wardrobe when she was always on an airplane or a train. She gave a sensible housewife's answer: "When I get back to Washington, I'll take these clothes I've been wearing to the dry cleaners. Since he doesn't work Saturdays, I'll have to wait until next week to get them, but I can pick up some that I left for cleaning the last time I was home. Then I'll be ready to join Lyndon in Missouri."

It was Bobby, Jack Kennedy's campaign manager, who summed up the extent of Lady Bird's efforts in the close-fought battle: "Lady Bird carried Texas for us." Coming from Bobby, that was no small admission.

However, there was one incident in Texas that caused Lady Bird much heartache. It was also a shocking prelude of events to come. During the last days of the campaign she arrived in Dallas with Lyndon, only to be involved in a terrible mob scene. Placards declaring TRAITOR bobbed up and down in their faces. Lyndon was accused of selling out his native South. Well-dressed men and women started to spit and scream. Somebody roughed up Lady Bird's hair. Through it all, husband and wife remained perfectly calm.

"I couldn't believe this was Texas," said Lady Bird afterward. "I couldn't believe this was home, where I had gone to school as a girl. But," she added kindly, "it was only a small segment of Dallas."

Afterward there was some compensation in knowing that thousands of other Texans were disgusted with the mob's behavior. Best of all, Texas went Democrat!

The new Second Lady in the land defined her position as "Helping Lyndon all I can, helping Mrs. Kennedy whenever she needs me, and becoming a more alive me."

She was a godsend to Mrs. Kennedy, who was still recuperating from the birth of John Jr. Often she sat opposite President Kennedy at the White House when important official visitors were being entertained. Later she did the same when Mrs. Kennedy was at one of her summer homes or traveling in foreign lands. Next to Jacqueline, she became the most important hostess in Washington. Between them they supplanted the society party-givers.

Now Lady Bird herself was president of the Senate Ladies' Red Cross Unit . . . and in order to be of more use to Lyndon she decided to study another language. Three mornings a week were taken up with learning to speak Spanish, Professor Elsa López McGuire being her teacher.

The Johnsons had grown out of Lady Bird's first dream house, and, in order to accede to President Kennedy's wishes that they help entertain official foreign visitors, they bought Les Ormes, the beautiful French château, from their friend Perle Mesta. At the President's request, Lady Bird entertained the Empress Farah of Iran and Indira Gandhi, daughter of Indian Prime Minister Nehru and now herself Prime Minister of India.

Mrs. Mesta, with her usual good taste, had brought gardeners and decorators from Paris to add their best talents to the already elegant house.

The Johnsons anglicized the name of their new abode to The Elms, hung their beloved Salinas paintings in places of honor, and remodeled the kitchen—but not before thrifty Lady Bird had carefully studied her usual three bids. There was also an office for Lady Bird. The Vice President was well provided for in this direction by his new suites in the Executive office building next to the White House and in the Capitol itself. Nevertheless, when at home he could not resist the urge to spread his papers all over the large double bed.

Lady Bird's office was a personal godsend, for her fan mail had increased 100 per cent.

When, in 1961, forty-one women delegates from thirty-two of the United Nations countries arrived from New York to meet the President while Mrs. Kennedy was away, although it was only a few days to Christmas, Lady Bird invited them all to tea at The Elms. The women were charmed with the decorations—old-fashioned mistletoe hanging from the sparkling crystal chandeliers, garlands of evergreens and a little pine tree festooned with silver.

The newly installed swimming pool made an informal meeting place for official visitors, friends, and Lynda Bird's and Luci's teen-age friends.

Little Beagle Johnson, of course, moved to the The Elms where he lived until his death from suspected poisoning in June of 1963. He had long since found his place in American canine history along with such celebrities as President Franklin D. Roosevelt's Fala and Vice President Nixon's Checkers.

All his life Little Beagle was prone to adventure. Once when he had decided to take off on his own for a vacation he was on the FBI's most wanted list. For some years he held the District of Columbia's number two license tag until the Kennedys' dogs demoted him to fourth.

The family were heartbroken when Little Beagle died. He was cremated and his ashes taken back to the ranch for burial. His son and daughter, offspring of another Texan beagle, returned to Washington with the family that fall.

"Daddy wouldn't let them put those little puppies in the baggage compartment," says Luci, "so I held one, and he held the other all the way. He kept petting and stroking it, so it wouldn't get scared, and Daddy even slept with the dog on top of him."

Luci soon named the new members of the Johnson family Him and Her. The latter's little life was short. On November 29, 1964, Lyndon announced at a press conference, "We have had a tragedy." Her had died on the operating table after swallowing a rock in the White House grounds. "Luci," he added, "is heartbroken about Her."

Shortly afterward Luci Baines Johnson sent me (I own an English beagle named Charmaine) this sensitive little letter:

> The White House
> Washington
> January 18, 1965

Dear Mr. Hall:

My family and I are touched by your sympathetic message about the loss of our beagle "Her." We will always remember her special little ways when expressing her love.

We all join in sending our thanks for your warm, kind words.

> Sincerely,
> Luci

Him's life was also destined to be short, though like his predecessor Little Beagle he left the Johnsons with his own special memories.

On June 15, 1966, while chasing a squirrel in the White House grounds, he ran beneath the wheels of a car. In tears Lynda Bird reported the news to her father. A Secret Service agent broke the news to Mrs. Johnson, who was taking part in a parade at Lincoln, Nebraska. She later told reporters that such news "makes you feel like you have been hit in the stomach by a rock."

Among Lady Bird's most rewarding achievements as Second Lady were the friendships she made while abroad with Lyndon upon official government business. Representing the United States at Senegal's independence celebrations, she made a point of carefully studying the country beforehand. Finding that new nation harvested millions of tons of peanuts each year, she felt on home ground, for her father had grown peanuts upon his plantation.

The American Ambassador's wife was amazed when Lady Bird set out to inspect a peanut farm. Even visiting Russians were outdone by the American Vice President and his wife, who felt naturally at ease visiting the crowded markets and streets, shaking hands, and exchanging greetings.

"Senegal is so breathtakingly brilliant in the array of people, languages, costumes, and customs that one tries to absorb it like a sponge," Lady Bird wrote home to a Washington newspaper.

Lady Bird's knowledge of shorthand was of immense help for note-taking upon these trips. In India Lyndon couldn't visit that greatest memorial to love, the Taj Mahal, without spontaneously kissing his wife right in the middle of the mausoleum. The usually precise State Department had forgotten to tell him that kissing in public is frowned upon by Indians.

In Pakistan Lady Bird was off on her own goodwill mission, inspecting hospitals and schools, in which field she was enormously successful. In Taipei, with Mrs. Chew Cheng, wife of the Vice President of Formosa, she went for a pedicab ride wearing a flowered straw hat.

The controversial Madame Nhu took Lady Bird to the Vietnamese Parliament, where she was introduced to feminine members of the National Assembly. Of Madame Nhu, the acutely discerning Lady Bird wrote:

"She's an intense, courageous, political personality, but what direction it [the political situation] will take I don't know."

Speaker Sam Rayburn died during November of 1961. They planned to fly to the funeral of Lyndon's old and cherished friend when word was received that Tony, Lady Bird's only surviving brother, had suffered a heart attack. After Lyndon had personally asked his own heart specialist, Dr. Willis Hurst of Atlanta, to fly to Tony's bedside, he arranged for Lady Bird's transportation. He kept saying, "You only have one brother."

"Lyndon's a good man to have around in an emergency," was her now-famous reply. He attended Mr. Sam's funeral on his own, insisting that Lady Bird be where she was most needed, and Tony Taylor eventually made a good recovery, just as Lyndon had done.

In 1962 Lady Bird accompanied her husband upon other diplomatic friendship missions overseas. They attended the independence celebrations in Jamaica, where Lady Bird was amused to note that a Lady So-and-So's signature preceded hers in a hotel register. Mischievously she signed "Lady Bird Johnson."

They were in Puerto Rico for its tenth commonwealth anniversary, and then came a wonderful trip to Greece and the Middle East, accompanied by Lynda Bird. Iran made them all nostalgic for Texas, so Lady Bird bought a large copper tray to give the Camp Fire Girls back in Marshall, Texas. In Athens the Vice President's wife was intrigued by a playground for children, converted from a grim former walled prison by Queen Frederika, whom America's Second Lady called "a working career Queen."

Childhood days at the Brick House in Karnack, with her mother, and Aunt Effie's tales from the Greek classics were vividly recalled when Lady Bird actually gave an address at the Acropolis. Even Lyndon was jolted by Lynda Bird's announcement: "As mother was saying when she spoke at the Acropolis today. . . ."

When like any other tourist she found herself asking,

"How old is that?" a guide mischievously answered, "Mrs. Johnson, everything here is B.C. except you and me."

Lynda accompanied her mother to the Smyrna of Biblical days, now known as Ismir, Turkey, to visit a girls' school of particular American interest, having been founded by Congregational Church women missionaries from New England.

Turkish women asked Lady Bird, "Do American women dominate men?" only to be reassured with a smile, "No, they're partners."

That April the seven astronauts arrived for a visit at the LBJ Ranch, signing their names in wet cement by the swimming pool. Later in Washington Lady Bird told their wives, "I think your husbands soon felt just as much at home on the range as in outer space."

The swimming pool at The Elms was the scene of an equally successful party given for a group of exchange students en route to the University of Chile.

Lady Bird, particularly interested in the welfare of students, wanted to share her "front row Capitol seat" with them. In her opinion, these young people who would be America's goodwill ambassadors were as important as the foreign aid program, which she once called "bread cast upon the waters which, as the Bible says, comes back tenfold in friendship for the United States."

She suggested that Americans entertain students and ordinary visiting tourists, saying, "My feeling is that every American can add to the friendly footprints of his country, even if he never leaves home."

Early in 1963 Lady Bird was carrying a schedule that was enough for five women. For example, on March 1 in West Virginia she visited unemployed coal miners being trained for new occupations, inspected projects that would boost the state's sagging economy, and went to a governor's reception followed by a banquet for Democratic women. Next day she flew to Detroit, where Lyndon was waiting, to attend a Jefferson-Jackson Day dinner and to meet women dignitaries.

For sheer energy and getting things done, only Eleanor Roosevelt could match her.

"I guess I married politics the day I married Lyndon," she said, preferring to be on hand to hear his more important speeches. Like the late Queen Mary, who tapped her parasol when her husband's speech was too long, whispering, "That's enough, George," Lady Bird can tell Lyndon when to stop.

In Baytown, Texas, that August, when his voice turned husky and he still did not end his speech, she scribbled the words "It's time to stop," and the Vice President did.

Lynda Bird once more accompanied her parents upon a goodwill mission, this time to Iceland and the Scandinavian countries. Because of her interest in agriculture, Lady Bird was an immediate success in Sweden. . . . At Bodo, Norway, they found a sign: NORTH POLE—three hours; LBJ RANCH—thirteen hours and forty-five minutes.

At the airport of the nineteen-year-old town, the predecessor of which had been leveled in World War II by the Nazis, the Vice Presidential party was met by a large crowd who later followed them upon bicycles.

A little Finnish girl led Lady Bird by the hand through the woods to show America's Second Lady where she went to collect the milk. The child delighted her with stories of the fairies and pixies who inhabited the flowers and trees. Spellbound, the clock turned back for Lady Bird . . . she thought of the little girl she had once been, walking with Aunt Effie in the woods around the Brick House.

No President or Vice President of the United States had

ever paid a goodwill visit to these countries before. It was a small triumph.

Yet with all the exciting events that crowded her days, Lady Bird could still find time to worry because back at the ranch she hadn't had time to tidy her closets as she would have liked . . . had time with Lyndon to save Abraham Lincoln's White House appointments book which they purchased in Boston as a gift for the Executive Mansion . . . had time to put up her peach preserves.

"I often think of that funny old sign on my daddy's store," she once said. "T. J. TAYLOR, DEALER IN EVERYTHING. That's not only the story of my life, but the story of America as well."

11

A Drift of Pink . . . .

* *

LADY BIRD was delighted that at last Jacqueline Kennedy was to visit the LBJ Ranch. The President had already sampled the hospitality of the Johnsons' Texas home, but at that time Jacqueline was pregnant and could not accompany him. Tennessee Walking Horse, Lady Bird's favorite, then training in the state for which it was named, would be back in time for Jacqueline's visit. Jacqueline, whose love for horses is universally known, would have a special show of whip cracking and quarter-horse cutting arranged in her honor.

Early on that fateful Friday, November 22, 1963, Lady Bird's helpers had been baking pies in preparation for the Kennedys' arrival. As the cavalcade drove through the streets of Dallas, Lady Bird found herself wondering how the pies had turned out . . . and if her guests liked home-grown pecans.

It was a beautiful day: the skies were blue and the crowds particularly friendly. She quickly put aside the memory of that awful day when a Dallas mob had spat upon Lyndon and herself. Just a week earlier the United States Ambassador to the United Nations, quiet, gentle-manly Adlai Stevenson, had been shamefully mistreated in

Dallas. He had even sent the President a warning to avoid the city but, on second thought, withdrew it. He did not think it fair to pass judgment upon an entire community because of the behavior of a few extremists.

Lady Bird, happy to be back in her native state, was sitting between her husband and Senator Ralph W. Yarborough of Texas two cars behind the Kennedys' own. Again she thought of the pies and of the fresh fruit she had placed in the guest rooms. It was 12:26 P.M.

Two minutes later the Presidential motorcade slowed down to make a sharp turn as it was approaching a triple underpass. A minute later Lady Bird heard three shots. At the time she thought they were firecrackers. . . . The occupants of the lead car seemed to have dropped from sight.

"Let's get out of here!" came the order over the intercom car radio. Her heart seemed to miss a beat as Secret Service Agent Rufus Youngblood, who was in the front of their car, leapt to the back, throwing himself across Lyndon and pushing him to the floor.

"Get down!" he shouted at Lady Bird and Senator Yarborough.

They crouched and lowered their heads, all that was possible in such limited space. Then the car lurched forward, gathering speed as it followed the others in front. As their car swerved into a driveway she looked up to read PARKLAND HOSPITAL and was gripped with a terrible foreboding of evil.

"Oh, my God," said Senator Yarborough. "Have they shot the President?"

"No," she managed to answer reassuringly. "I don't think that can be."

Now someone was hustling her out of the car while a medley of frightened voices came from all directions: "It's terrible, terrible. . . . There's a terrible plot. . . . Somebody's shot the President. . . . Governor Connally's shot too."

For one dreadful moment she had seen "a drift of pink

—like pink blossoms" in the car in front. . . . She thought later it was Mrs. Kennedy, shielding the body of her husband.

Secret Service men seemed to be everywhere, as the visitors were bustled through the hospital doors and along a maze of corridors. Then Lyndon's party was inside a small room, with white sheet-lined walls that seemed to be closing in upon them. Suddenly she knew that she had to find Jacqueline Kennedy, so the Secret Service men helped her.

They found her quite alone yet utterly composed, standing outside of the operating room. Lady Bird has recorded that never in her life had she ever wanted so much to comfort anyone, yet never before had felt so helpless. . . . It was the younger woman's calmness in the midst of tragedy that amazed her, yet, says Lady Bird, "when you looked at her eyes you could almost die!"

For a moment all the motherly-sisterly instinct that is so much part of Lady Bird Johnson's makeup came to the fore. . . . She put out both arms and comforted Jacqueline, who managed to whisper, "We had ten years together . . ." then smiled, for as Lady Bird said later, "We both knew that we were trying."

Then Lady Bird went to find her old and cherished friend, Nellie Connally, wife of the Governor of Texas who had been seriously injured in the shooting. Somebody remarked that he was not expected to live. Nellie seemed to fall into her arms and they were weeping together. At 1:16 P.M. Lady Bird returned to Lyndon's side. She choked back a sob as White House Press Secretary Malcolm Kilduff addressed him as "Mr. President."

John F. Kennedy was dead. . . .

"I have to announce the death of President Kennedy to the press." Kilduff was speaking to Lyndon. "Is it all right with you?" At that moment Lady Bird felt part of one of those Greek tragedies she had read so often as a girl.

"No, Mac," replied President Kennedy's successor. "I think we had better wait for a few minutes. I think I had better get out of here and get back to the plane before you announce it. . . . We don't know whether this is a world-wide conspiracy, and whether they are after me as well as they were after President Kennedy. . . . We just don't know."

Meanwhile, the Attorney General of the United States, Robert Kennedy, the late President's brother, advised them by telephone that the swearing-in of the new President should take place in the plane at the airfield. Even in the midst of great personal sorrow the wheels of government must continue to turn.

A few minutes later they were ushered into a closed car and taken to the airport, where they boarded Air Force One. When a Secret Service man, fearing further trouble, suggested leaving Love Field at once, the new President said with a quiet finality, "No, we will wait for Mrs. Kennedy and Mr. Kennedy's body."

Lady Bird felt only what she calls "an infinite compassion" at that moment.

While her husband made various telephone calls from the Presidential cabin, Lady Bird began to make notes, while the facts were fresh in her mind, of her own role in that day's ghastly happenings. Lyndon was now part of history and she was part of Lyndon. She steeled herself to reconstruct each tragic detail. . . .

At 2:25 P.M., Judge Sarah Hughes arrived, carrying a Bible to administer the Presidential oath. Lady Bird noticed the grim lines of shock etched upon Lyndon's forehead. She moved to his right side but the ceremony did not begin at once, for Jacqueline Kennedy, who had now arrived, was composing herself. . . . When she came back Lady Bird gave a faint smile of encouragement. Lyndon took the former First Lady by the hands and gently guided her to a place of honor on his left side. Then their longtime friend, Judge Hughes, administered the oath. Lady Bird felt strengthened as Lyndon answered, "So help me God," knowing that he meant it. How she wished Rebekah, his mother, were there to add her encouragement and blessings—yet wasn't she there in spirit?

When it was over the new President kissed his wife upon the forehead . . . and then he kissed Jacqueline. With authority he ordered, "Okay, let's get this plane back to Washington."

"The whole nation mourns your husband," Lady Bird whispered as she took Jacqueline's cold hands in her own.

Lady Bird cannot remember if they were served hot bouillon or coffee, for a sense of numbness was setting in. Lyndon had one more important thing to do: he had to reassure a shocked America.

"This is a sad time for all people," he said in his first public statement, dictated on the plane. "We have suffered a loss that cannot be weighed. For me it is a deep personal tragedy. I know the world shares the sorrow that Mrs. Kennedy and her family bear. I will do my best. That is all I can do. I ask for your help—and God's."

How grateful Lady Bird was when at last her car sped through the gates of The Elms and they closed behind her! She was alone now; Lyndon was conferring in the Vice Presidential offices at the Executive Building close by the White House. She was somewhat startled to be informed by a Secret Service man that the White House telephone numbers had replaced her own.

Luci was already standing on the front steps to greet her. Both near tears, they kissed each other. Luci was saying: "Oh, Mother, at school Miss Lee called me in and told me. And then all the girls said a prayer for Daddy."

There had been a crowd of reporters waiting outside those gates that had previously always been left open. Elizabeth Carpenter took them a message from Lady Bird. "It seems like a dreadful nightmare," she had said. "Somehow we must find the strength to go on."

Meanwhile the First Lady was watching a newscast of the day's events on television. Once more she was struck by their resemblance to a classic Greek tragedy. Then she went upstairs and changed the favorite beige dress she was wearing for a green hostess robe.

Next came a call to Lynda Bird at the University of Texas. How her heart glowed when the young girl exclaimed, "Mother, the first thing I did when I heard the news was go to the Governor's mansion to be with the Connally children."

Lady Bird remembered that Lyndon had not eaten, so she asked that plenty of his favorite fried chicken be prepared. She felt sure there would be others with him. Then she rested until 9:24 P.M., when news came that he was on the way home. She patted her hair into place and went down to meet him.

The President wasn't hungry for in the rush of immediate business he had forgotten to call and let her know that someone had brought him a hamburger. With several of his staff he retired to the terrace room where she, with a plate of fried chicken, joined them.

There were more newscasts; then at midnight Lady Bird went up to bed. As she undressed she could only think of that look in Jacqueline Kennedy's eyes.

Downstairs, a short while before, somebody had asked what she had said to Jacqueline.

"How do you know what you say at such a time? You just say what you hope and pray will give comfort," had been her answer.

Next morning Lady Bird was up early. Dressed in black

she was talking to the staff when in walked her personal secretary, Bess Abell. She had been at the LBJ Ranch making last-minute arrangements for the Kennedys' visit when she heard of the President's death. She had flown immediately to Dallas, then on to Washington, arriving at 6 A.M.

"Oh, poor, poor Bess," sympathized Lady Bird. "You've just had no sleep at all!"

At 10:20 A.M. Lady Bird joined Lyndon at his office where Congressional leaders of both parties were gathering with their wives to walk through the rain to the White House. She walked with Lyndon past the flag-draped casket in the historic East Room and thought of another martyred President who had rested there: Abraham Lincoln. She went upstairs to the family quarters for a brief visit with Jacqueline while Lyndon stayed behind to talk with former President Eisenhower, who at that moment seemed such a tower of strength to them all.

Jacqueline seemed as much concerned over Lady Bird's welfare as Lady Bird had been over hers. Lady Bird repeated several times that the former First Lady was to be in no hurry to move. Then she joined Lyndon for a service in St. John's Episcopal Church, affectionately known as the "Church of the Presidents," because, since the era of President James Madison, each of his successors had at some time worshiped there.

Lady Bird, an Episcopalian, felt strengthened by the simple, dignified prayers, especially when the rector, the Reverend John Harper, asked, "O, God, bless Thy servant Lyndon and all others in authority so they may always do Thy will."

Home again, she called Governor Connally's wife. Nellie was trying to sound her old cheerful self when asked about her husband.

"Well, he's still critical, but he's not critically critical," she said. Then she asked how Lyndon was doing.

"Oh, he's just wonderful," replied Lady Bird. "He's staying up later, and getting up earlier, and thinking of everything before the rest of us do."

From the moment she became First Lady under such tragic circumstances, letters and telegrams poured in from well-wishers everywhere. There were over 200,000 letters, which worried her, because she could not possibly answer so many herself, but, said she, "My friends will think it mighty strange if I don't."

It was then that a wonderful group of Congressional wives and other friends solved her problem. They came in relays to the The Elms to answer the vast correspondence. To express her thanks she gave each of them a tiny crystal bird found during the official trip with Lyndon to Scandinavia.

Lynda Bird came home to ease her mother's burden. Both girls were a very real help.

On President Kennedy's funeral day Lady Bird rode beside her husband in the procession from the Capitol to the White House. Then, against the wishes of the Secret Service men, they walked six blocks from the White House to St. Matthew's Cathedral.

After the late President's burial in Arlington National Cemetery, Lady Bird returned alone to The Elms as Lyndon was greeting important overseas mourners at an all-male reception. At 4 P.M. she had just sat down to lunch when a call came through from Chief of Protocol Angier Biddle Duke that Lyndon would like her to come and help him with the lady visitors.

Leaving her meal untouched, she returned immediately to the White House to talk with Queen Frederika of

Greece, Crown Princess Beatrix of Holland, Madam Pandit of India, and many others. . . .

"I wish to heaven I could serve Mrs. Kennedy's happiness. . . . I can at least serve her convenience. I have had considerable experience in innumerable moves of children, pets, and household things, and I know what moving involves. It is only when the last chore she wishes to do is done that I will contemplate moving."

Lady Bird Johnson, her heart still overflowing for Mrs. Kennedy, and mindful of traveling with her own family between Washington and Texas, made this statement even before her predecessor had sent J. B. West, the head White House Usher, to brief her upon the running of the nation's first home. In addition, Jacqueline prepared a handwritten memorandum, running to five legal-size pages, that listed formal White House plans and events for the near future.

Mrs. Kennedy, from the moment of that brief intimate meeting at the hospital in Dallas, had shown a sympathetic concern for the problems of her successor. She invited Lady Bird to talk over the Executive Mansion's restoration plans and to visit the family quarters so that Lady Bird could make some plans of her own. She completely agreed with Jacqueline's suggestion that little Caroline Kennedy's school with its class of twenty-one children ages five and six might meet as usual upon the third floor until the Christmas recess. Both President and Mrs. Johnson made it their business to visit the children and greet each one individually.

Thanksgiving that year was spent at The Elms instead of at the LBJ Ranch. They seemed to miss their Texas home more than ever. Lynda Bird returned to the University of Texas, worried at the cost of telephone calls, because now that they would be living in the White House it would be impossible to call her parents station to station. Back at the university, she had the new experience of having Secret Service agents on duty to guard her. Photographers' cameras seemed everywhere.

Luci, like her sister, had adapted herself well to the strange new situation. The day after President Kennedy's funeral she did not forget to take her share of groceries to help fill her school's Thanksgiving boxes.

Both girls had sat with their mother in the "family gallery" of the United States Capitol to hear Lyndon give his first address as President to a joint session of Congress. Their presence gave him added courage for the tasks ahead.

The day before she moved into the White House, Lady Bird paid one of the most beautiful tributes ever made to another woman when she said: "Jacqueline Bouvier Kennedy leaves a shining gift of beauty in this historic house. At every turn we are freshly conscious of our heritage. The most knowledgeable expert, as well as the busloads of school children who visit, will always know that a young and radiant First Lady lived here. We know her better than ever before, and hold her close to our hearts with inexpressible pride."

The Elms was put up for sale; Lady Bird had also applied to the Federal Communications Commission for permission to transfer her successful radio holdings to a trusteeship.

On the afternoon of December 7, the new First Lady arrived at the White House clutching her favorite portrait of the late Sam Rayburn to hang in the family sitting room. With her went the domestic staff: Mrs. Zephyr Wright, whose new kitchen had once been the location of Margaret Truman's bedroom; Mrs. Helen Williams, the housekeeper and formerly the girls' nursemaid, and Mrs. Lee Gregg.

Elizabeth Carpenter and Bess Abell traveled in the same car as the First Lady. They made an efficient team.

On arrival she found a bouquet of flowers and a letter of welcome from Jacqueline Kennedy, who had moved temporarily into a stately red brick Georgian-style house at 3038 N Street, lent her by Undersecretary of State E. Averell Harriman and Mrs. Harriman.

From a tiny one-bedroom apartment when she had come to Washington as Lyndon's bride, Lady Bird Johnson was now chatelaine of America's first home, with a household budget amounting to $670,000. Even her father Cap and her uncle Claude Pattillo would have been a little overwhelmed at the sum, although with the training they had given her they would have known she could cope.

Yet First Lady or not, she would never forget her other roles as wife and mother. "I will try," vowed Lady Bird, "to be balm, sustainer, and sometimes critic for my husband. I will try to help my children look at this job with all the reverence it is due, to get from it the knowledge their unique vantage point gives them, and to retain the lightheartedness to which every teen-ager is entitled. For my own self my role must emerge in deeds, not words."

In the busy months that followed, those deeds more than adequately spoke for themselves.

Christmas was sadly strange and silent. Flags were still flying at half mast for President Kennedy. It was now Lady Bird's duty, as First Lady in the land, to emphasize the real meaning of Christmas. It was the children's time. It must not be spoiled.

On December 11 she fulfilled a promise made to Jacqueline Kennedy, personally distributing gifts to patients in the Children's Wing of the District of Columbia General Hospital. Luci, good with youngsters, accompanied her mother as each child recieved a gift tied with a red ribbon. Sometimes the First Lady was asked for her autograph, giving it with a smile. Then there was a White House ballet performance to be arranged for a hundred and fifty underprivileged children. In between she visited her old home, The Elms, where she would suddenly see knickknacks that she would decide she must have at the White House. She turned the little dressing room that had been Jacqueline Kennedy's into her office.

National mourning for John F. Kennedy ended on Lady Bird's birthday. That evening President Johnson spoke during a moving candlelight service held at the Lincoln Memorial. Later a crowd in the street spontaneously sang, "Happy birthday, dear Lady Bird, happy birthday to you."

Then it was time for the two Christmas trees—the Nation's very own tree at the ellipse behind the White House, which was lighted by Lyndon, and their own glittering symbol of the festive season in the White House.

The White House tree resembled a dazzling cone of light in the oval Blue Room. The mourning crêpe was gone; peace and goodwill seemed at least temporarily to have crept back into the world.

A group of women reporters were amused by the mistletoe kissing ball that hung from a crystal chandelier in the dining room, a reminder of Lady Bird's Southern childhood. The President gave the First Lady his portrait, signed, as he had once signed another twenty-nine years before, "For Bird, a girl of principles, ideals, and refinement, from her admirer, Lyndon."

They arrived home in Texas on Christmas Eve, first visiting Governor John Connally to see the good progress he was making. At the LBJ Ranch, twenty-seven relatives joined them for a turkey dinner, but not before Lyndon had introduced them all to some sixty reporters and photographers. All Lady Bird could think about was her turkey that threatened to spoil.

That Friday the representatives of the press were back in force, five busloads of them, for a grand tour of the ranch.

Lady Bird was one of the guides, using a microphone to outline points of interest. Later the President spoke from the top of two bales of hay, while Lady Bird went straight to the newsmen's hearts with her spareribs and draft beer.

On New Year's Day in Texas, Lady Bird served traditional Southern black-eyed peas, while back at the White House Mrs. Dean Rusk took her place as hostess to underprivileged children at a performance of the Dutch Scappino Ballet given January 2. On Twelfth Night Lady Bird shook more than a thousand hands at the party given to White House staffers and their families. . . . For Lyndon's first State of the Union address to Congress she took Helen Williams, her housekeeper, to sit with her in the Family Gallery, just as she had taken Zephyr Wright, the cook, to hear him address his first joint session.

At the end of the week Lady Bird flew to Wilkes-Barre, Pennsylvania, to give at Wilkes College a speech that she herself had written and to tour the frontline area for an on-the-spot look at what her husband was fighting in his newly declared war on poverty.

Clutching a baby under her arm, one young mother ran through an icy street to clasp the First Lady's hand. "She's such a real person," she afterward explained. "She really feels concern for the unemployed."

There in the long-depressed anthracite coal regions of Pennsylvania Lady Bird stood in snow-covered public squares to address the crowds of miners' wives, garment workers, teachers, and students. LBJ's LADY BIRD read the welcoming posters.

At Wilkes College she met educators endeavoring to teach an entire community new skills to replace the old ones lost with the deserted coal mines. She told a man training as a house painter that she did her own painting on the ranch, mixing her own paints.

"The one thing we cannot afford is poverty," she declared. "The problems here are not the problems of party. Poverty affects all of us. All must enlist in this war against poverty, and all of us must work together." Women in the crowd called her a second Eleanor Roosevelt.

This visit to Appalachia starred a new Lady Bird: the new First Lady with the common touch who could be as much at home speaking to a poor woman and her baby as entertaining Queen Frederika of Greece or Princess Margaret of Great Britain in the glittering splendor of the Executive Mansion.

Following the pattern laid down by Eleanor Roosevelt, she would see firsthand the slums of Appalachia and Harlem.

She was beginning to make her own image live—to be really and truly First Lady.

Living in the shadow of Jacqueline Kennedy, Mrs. Johnson had no easy path to tread when it came to establishing her own personality in the White House. For example, one veteran White House staff member had the disturbing habit of constantly interrupting his guided tours to point out Mrs. Kennedy's favorite paintings and furnishings.

"Ah, this is Mrs. Kennedy's favorite portrait," he would say, gazing at Angelica Van Buren's portrait by Henry Inman in the Green Room. In the historic East Room he would pause to impart the information that the former First Lady was so fond of it that "she didn't have the heart to change the decor."

Mrs. Johnson's preferences in paintings and furnishings were never mentioned, so that a visitor would wonder if she really lived there.

Fortunately Lady Bird champions her predecessor's good taste and is glad that there is no need to compete with Jacqueline on this score. It never bothered her when thoughtless people told her "how well Jackie decorated the

White House, turning it from a mausoleum into a home."

While taking part in a color television program on the Executive Mansion's art collection, Lady Bird was asked, "What are your favorite portraits?" She paused for a moment as if to give the matter careful thought. "Why, I'm partial to the ones of Thomas Jefferson and Benjamin Franklin," she replied in her soft East Texas drawl. "And my goodness, I hope they are in the film."

They were.

For the first Senate wives' luncheon she presided over as First Lady, Lady Bird, who knows her White House history, arranged this "historic" menu:

Hayes Melon Cup, Veal Abigail Adams, Rice Pilaf First Lady, Asparagus Monticello, Strawberry Sherbet Dolley Madison, and Demitasse.

Of the famous White House collection of executive china, she considered the Lincoln service to be "among the handsomest, with its impressive royal purple border," and thought the Benjamin Harrison china with its goldenrod and corn motif to most signify the "bounty of this land."

Once a week Lady Bird quietly made a record of current events as she had personally lived them. Except for the excerpt she released for the Warren Report concerning the assassination of President Kennedy, only nineteen-year-old Scott Carpenter, son of Elizabeth Carpenter, heard them. Until the Army provided the First Lady with an easy-to-operate recorder, Scott came to the rescue with his $12 Japanese machine. They made some fifteen hour-long tapes together, because Lady Bird found the machine too tricky to operate herself. Scott respected Mrs. Johnson's confidence concerning the contents.

As his mother said: "At first, after the assassination, she was recording every day. She didn't want anybody to know, not even the President. She would just call Scott up on the phone and tell him to bring his machine over as quickly as he could. In those days of heavy strain, I think it was good therapy. Now, although she doesn't plan ever to publish her words, Mrs. Johnson keeps up with it because she has an acute sense of history."

Lady Bird soon joined the other First Ladies in the Smithsonian Institution, Washington. Her effigy wears the same rich golden satin gown that in real life graced a State Dinner given for Britain's Prime Minister Harold Wilson. There is a matching satin stole.

"She" stands next to a figure representing Jacqueline Kennedy that displays her inaugural gown of white peau d'ange veiled with chiffon for a soft shimmering effect.

Mamie Eisenhower's first inaugural ball gown of Renoir pink peau de soie was designed by Nettie Rosenstein of New York. It is heavily embroidered with pink rhinestones. Lady Bird, Jacqueline, and Mamie make a pleasing trio.

12

Southern First Ladies

* *

SOME of the most interesting and colorful of America's First Ladies have, like Lady Bird Johnson, been Southerners.

The first of them, Martha Dandridge Custis Washington (1732–1802), sometimes known as the Mother of Our Country, never lived in the White House, as it was not completed during her lifetime. However, she did live at the time of her marriage to Washington in "The White House" on the York River in Virginia.

She was a rich and comely widow when they first met. Her first husband, Daniel P. Custis, had died in 1757, leaving her with two children, two others having been lost in infancy. (Her father-in-law was that same John Custis who had obtained a posthumous revenge upon his shrewish wife Frances by the epitaph he ordered to be engraved upon his tomb: "Aged 71 years and yet lived but seven years which was the space of time he kept a bachelor's house at Arlington on the eastern shores of Virginia.")

The wedding took place on January 6, 1759, whether in church or at the bride's home being unknown. For her wedding the twenty-seven-year-old bride wore a quilted petticoat of white satin, over which was a heavy corded silk skirt with ruffles and point lace. Diamond buckles sparkled from her white satin slippers. Her necklace, bracelet, and earrings were of pearls, and there were pearl ornaments in her hair.

On May 1, Washington sent the London agents of the Custis property "the minister's certificate of my marriage with Mrs. Martha Custis, properly, as I am told, authenticated." Custis had left Martha securities to the value of $33,500, an immense sum in those days, which according to law immediately became the property of her new husband. To his children, Martha and John Custis, their father had left each an equal sum, Washington serving as their trustee.

The newlyweds settled at Washington's own plantation, Mount Vernon, from where he wrote an English relative, "I am now, I believe, fixed in this spot with an agreeable partner for life; and I hope to find more happiness in retirement than I ever experienced in the wide and bustling world."

The Washingtons were noted for their bountiful hospitality, so that George once saw fit to note in his diary, "Would anyone believe that with 101 cows . . . I should still be obliged to buy butter for my family?"

Martha's happiness was marred by the death of her beloved daughter, Martha Parke Custis, which took place in 1773. A year later, her son John married Eleanor Calvert, but Martha was still too overwrought with grief to attend the ceremony. Instead she wrote the bride:

My dear Nelly—
God took from Me a Daughter when June roses were blooming. He has given me another daughter about her age when Winter winds are blowing, to warm my Heart again. . . . Pray receive my Benedic-

tion and a wish that you may long live the Loving
Wife of my happy Son, and a Loving Daughter.

Your affectionate Mother,
M. Washington

On December 16, 1773, occurred the famous Boston
Tea Party, and during the months that followed the American patriots determined the course that was to shape the
destiny of their country. "I hope that you will stand firm—I
know that George will," she told Edmund Pendleton and
Patrick Henry as they set out to attend a general Congress
in Philadelphia. "My mind is made up. My heart is in the
cause," she wrote a relative.

During the years of war and hardship that followed,
when George Washington led the American troops, she
faithfully served both her husband and his country.

To Martha he wrote, "I shall feel no pain from the toil
or danger of the campaign; my unhappiness will flow from
the uneasiness you will feel from being left alone. I there-
fore beg that you will summon your whole fortitude, and
pass your time as agreeably as possible."

She did not stay home for long, joining him in December
of 1775 at his Cambridge headquarters because he needed
her companionship. She was particularly helpful in bringing harmony to his quarreling officers by personally making friends with their wives.

Later, in March 1777, she journeyed through a wintry
countryside to his Morristown, New Jersey, headquarters,
where she nursed him back to health from a sickness,
cheered the forlorn camp, and organized officers' wives
into sewing groups to make clothing for the troops.

Expecting to find a grand lady, some Morristown women
called upon her. Their visit is best described by a certain
Mrs. Troupe, one of their number: "We dressed ourselves
in our most elegant ruffles and silks, and were introduced

to her ladyship . . . we found her knitting and with a specked apron on! There we were without a stitch of work and sitting in State, but General Washington's lady was knitting stockings."

Later, Martha would tell her grandchildren of how she had heard the opening and closing shot of nearly every important Revolutionary campaign.

With independence won, Martha Washington's service to her country was far from ended. General Washington was summoned to the Presidency in 1789, and she became First Lady.

"I had little thought when the war was finished," she confided to a friend, "that any circumstances could possibly happen which would call the General into public life again. I had anticipated, from that moment, we should be suffered to grow old together in solitude and tranquility. That was the first and dearest wish of my heart."

When after eight years Washington returned to private life at Mount Vernon, Martha happily wrote, "The General and I feel like children just released from school."

Dolley Dandridge Payne Todd Madison, one of the nation's most glamorous First Ladies, was born in what is now Guildford County, North Carolina. Even today people want to spell her name Dolly, although on the day she married James Madison she had twice spelt it Dolley in a letter which is now in the Library of Congress.

Raised as a Quaker and first wed to John Todd, a lawyer of that faith, Dolley lived happily with him for three years on South Fourth Street in Philadelphia. After his death from yellow fever she helped run her impoverished mother's boardinghouse where she met Aaron Burr, who introduced her to Jefferson's protégé, James Madison. Shy and reserved by nature, he was just the opposite to Dolley. When they married in 1794 it was with the approval of none other than Martha Washington herself!

Although Thomas Jefferson had not been happy when his protégé Madison wed Dolley, he was among the first to appreciate her common sense and charm. Often she served as his official hostess in the White House.

In 1809 when her husband succeeded Jefferson, Dolley's cuisine was patterned upon Jefferson's. She loved to serve French dishes, fine wines, macaroons, and ice cream. Ladies newly resident in Washington were first "presented to Her Majesty" in private before appearing at one of her official drawing rooms. A favorite jingle of the time was:

Tom Tingey, Tom Turner, Tom Elwell, Tom Digges,
All go to the palace to eat up the figs.

Dolley, who called her husband "my darling little husband," was three inches taller than he. Madison was also twenty years her senior. Mrs. William Seaton leaves this contemporary description of them both. "Her frank cordiality to all guests is in contrast to the manner of the President, who is very formal, reserved, and precise, though not wanting in a certain dignity. Being so low of stature, he was in imminent danger of being confounded with the plebian crowd, and was pushed and jostled like a common citizen—but not so her ladyship! The towering feathers and excessive throng pointed her station wherever she moved."

When Dolley bought herself a macaw, other women copied her. Aaron Burr thought it uncomely when she took snuff.

Political friends and foes of her husband were equally welcome at the White House. She expected them all to behave like civilized human beings. Their wives, after her husband became President, called her "Lady Presidentess" or "Her Majesty." When Mrs. Anthony Merry, wife of the British Minister, complained that Dolley's well-stocked table was "more like a harvest home supper than the entertainment of a Secretary of State," Dolley replied serenely,

"The profusion of my table, so repugnant to foreign customs, arises from the happy circumstances of abundance and prosperity in our country."

Dolley became a national heroine in 1812 when the British forces were advancing upon Washington. While her husband took over command at the front she stayed in the President's House almost to the hour that the enemy entered the city, August 24, 1814. Due to her sense of calm Gilbert Stuart's irreplaceable painting of George Washington was saved.

Like Lady Bird Johnson, Dolley left a record of her thoughts and emotions when history was being made. Wrote she:

"Two messengers, covered with dust, came to bid me fly—but here I mean to wait for him [her husband]— Our kind friend Mr. Carroll has come to hasten my departure and is in a very bad humor with me because I insist on waiting until the large picture of General Washington is secured, and it requires to be unscrewed from the wall. This process is found too tedious for these perilous moments; I have ordered the frame to be broken and the canvas taken out. It is done, and the precious portrait placed in the hands of two gentlemen of New York for safe keeping."

She also saved her macaw, one of the earliest pets ever known to have belonged to a First Family.

Of her character another woman said, "She is a strong-minded woman, fully capable of entering into her husband's occupations and cares." The same could have been written for Lady Bird.

"I had rather be a doorkeeper in the house of God than live in that palace in Washington," bemoaned Rachel Donelson Robards Jackson, most tragic—with the exception perhaps of Mary Todd Lincoln—of all Southern First Ladies. Rachel died of a heart attack before going to live in the White House and was buried on Christmas Eve, wearing her white satin inaugural gown, at the Hermitage, near Nashville, Tennessee.

Rachel, a child of the frontier who had braved Indians and the elements to pioneer a new home upon the site of what is now Nashville, was well suited to "Old Hickory," by which name dashing Andrew Jackson was popularly known.

When they had married in 1791, they had both believed that Rachel's former husband, Lewis Robards, had obtained a divorce from her for desertion. The frontier girl and the moody Robards were most unsuited to one another and had soon parted. However, Robards had only obtained permission from the Virginia Legislature, which then handled divorces, to sue in Kentucky. When he did sue for divorce it was in 1793 when the Jacksons had been "married" for two years, naming Jackson as correspondent and winning the case. The Jacksons were stunned. Quietly they went through a second ceremony to make their marriage legal.

With the years cementing a happy union, Tennessee seemingly forgot the incident, for Jackson was popular as a soldier and Rachel had endeared herself by reason of her good works in the community. She was always surrounded with young people, legally adopting a nephew, Andrew Jackson, Jr., and giving other nephews college educations and nieces weddings. Her one fear was Jackson's being called to participate in another military or political campaign.

Writing to a niece, she revealed: "In the thirty years of our wedded life he has not spent one-fourth of his days under his own roof. The rest of the time away, traveling, holding court, or at the capital of his country, or in camp, or fighting its battles, or treating [sic] with the Indians —mercy knows what not."

Jackson worshiped Rachel. To one of their nephews he said: "Recollect the industry of your dear aunt, and with what economy she watched over what I made, and how we waded through the vast expense of the mass of company we had. Nothing but her care and industry could have saved me from ruin."

When Jackson won the Presidency in 1828, Rachel, past sixty, said, "For Mr. Jackson's sake, I am glad; for my own part, I never wished it."

She had not enjoyed the two visits made to Washington in 1817, when the so-called fashionable ladies had looked down upon her frontier background with airs of superiority. However, for her husband's sake she bought an inaugural gown and wardrobe suitable for the White House. For the occasion, the ladies of Cincinnati, Ohio, gave her a beautiful lace veil upon which the name JACKSON was embroidered, with a star for each of the twenty-four states above the name.

While in Nashville, having fittings for the gown, she overheard rival political campaign gossip that she had been intimate with Andrew before their marriage, that she was socially inferior to him, that she would be a hindrance rather than a help at the White House. This preyed upon her mind, precipitating the heart attack that occurred on December 22.

A brokenhearted Jackson blamed Henry Clay and John Quincy Adams for Rachel's death and arrived in the capital for his inauguration with a heavy band of black crêpe upon his arm.

Bitterly he penned the epitaph for her tomb: A *being so gentle and virtuous, slander might wound but could not dishonor.*

Three years before President John Tyler came to the White House in 1841, his wife Letitia Christian Tyler, who had been born at Cedar Grove, New Kent County, Virginia, had suffered a paralytic stroke that had almost completely disabled her.

Only once did she appear in public at the White House and that was at the marriage of her youngest daughter, Elizabeth, to William Waller of Williamsburg, which took place in the East Room. Dolly Madison was among the brilliant assembly present. Mrs. Tyler wore "a quiet gown of faultless taste," her face "shaded by the soft lace of her cap."

Of Letitia, President Tyler told one of his children:

"I could not hold up for you a better pattern for your imitation than is constantly presented to you by your dear mother. You never saw her course marked with precipitation, but on the contrary, everything is brought before the tribunal of her judgement, and all her actions are founded in prudence."

As the eldest daughter, Letitia Temple, was nursing her mother, she was unable to act as First Lady in Mrs. Tyler's place. Until the older Letitia's death at fifty-one, September 10, 1842, the acting First Lady was a former actress, Elizabeth Priscilla Cooper Tyler, wife of Tyler's eldest son, Robert. She was the daughter of the great English tragedian, Thomas Apthorpe Cooper (of whom Washington Irving once said that no actor in England could equal his *Macbeth*), and of Mary Fairlie Cooper, that brilliant American woman called by Irving "the fascinating Fairlie." Irving made her the "Sophy Sparkle" of his *Salmagundi Papers*.

When Priscilla was appearing in *The Honeymoon* in Charleston, South Carolina, one performance was attended by Osceola, a Seminole Indian prisoner of war. He is said to have appreciated the sound of the trombone more than her acting. In any case, she found the presence of an Indian complete with war paint more than small competition.

President Tyler soon forgot the "prudent" Letitia. In 1844 he went to the altar at the Church of the Ascension, New York City, with Julia Gardiner, who was younger than some of his own children. She was appropriately known as the Rose of Long Island.

"Who is Polk?" the people asked in New England and in the Western territories. Until that time only men of great fame had been nominated for President, but this James K. Polk from Tennessee had the blessing of popular Andrew Jackson—"Old Hickory"—so the Democrats hopefully answered, "Young Hickory."

Polk was a worker and so was his wife, Sarah Childress Polk, who had been born September 4, 1803, in Murfreesboro, Tennessee. James and Sarah had always worked together as a team and when he was a young lawyer had discussed together his early cases. Now, when the Presidential nomination had been offered him, Sarah was ready to work quietly and thoroughly at winning the campaign.

A lady partial to the Elizabeth Barrett Browning type of corkscrew curls, she was determined to bring dignity to the White House. She had a great sense of history, so that although it poured with rain at her husband's inauguration she carried a fan depicting all the Presidents to date, so that it might become a historic relic.

She hated dancing and what she termed "worldly pleasures," so that the dancing stopped when, wearing "a mazarine blue velvet dress with a deeply fringed cape," she arrived at the Inauguration Ball.

Disliking gossip, she quickly contradicted rumors that young Julia Gardiner Tyler had left the White House in such a sorry state from their entertaining that the Polks would have to spend much good tax money to put it in shape again. New York's *Journal of Commerce* reported:

"A couple of upholsterers who went from this city to procure so much of the job as falls within their department came back with very reduced expectations. They were referred to the President's lady, who gave them a courteous interview of three-quarters of an hour, but told them only the public rooms would require repairs, for if the private apartments had been satisfactory to Mrs. Tyler, they would be so to herself."

Although in addition to dancing Sarah banned the serving of wines and liquors in the White House, she became the good friend of that Queen of Parties, Dolley Madison, who had been forced to leave her home, Montpelier, Virginia, because of reduced financial circumstances and now lived in a small house on the east side of Lafayette Square. Congress had given Dolley the highest honor yet given to a President's widow by voting her a lifetime seat on the floor of the House.

Sarah was interested in Dolley's plan to sell to the nation her husband's historic papers, which would ensure his widow a measure of security for the rest of her days. During May of 1848 a fire broke out in Dolley's house, so that she had to be rescued at four o'clock in the morning, after first seeing that her husband's papers were saved. Congress now realized that the papers had to be procured at once, passing a bill in which Dolley was to be given an appropriation of $25,000, to be kept in trust for her own security. The first thing she did was take her best silver forks out of pawn!

When gas lighting was installed in the White House, Sarah insisted that the reception hall "with its elegant chandelier for the use of candles" should be left unspoiled by the new discovery. In the years that followed she often told how on the first reception night, "Lo, the brilliant jets vanished and the company was left in darkness," yet there was "one room still lustrous with many points of light—the reception room where the wax candles were shedding their soft radiance."

James, disturbed that his hard-working Sarah might one day be reduced to poverty like Dolley Madison, helped plan the building of Polk Place, Nashville, in his will stipulating it be kept intact for her lifetime.

Dolley let the Polks copy the original Stuart paintings in her home, and they themselves were painted by George Healy. Mathew B. Brady, later to become famous as a photographer in the War between the States, made their daguerreotype seated together. These and other mementos of their tenure of the White House would later delight visitors to Polk Place.

Sarah never in her life played a card game or attended a horse race, and when her steamer was blown ashore she complained because a band came aboard on Sunday to entertain the stranded passengers, but despite this her public receptions were a great success. Believing that the American people had a right to meet their President, the Polks received them in the White House two evenings each week. Commented a contemporary, "It was known that he [the President] was in the habit of cutting off from his sleep the hours lost, to make up the amount of time which he felt belonged to the nation."

To save her husband valuable time, Sarah Polk read every available newspaper, marking sections on editorial opinion she thought he should see, as Lady Bird was to do later.

At their last reception the aged Dolley Madison was present, looking resplendent and "seated on a raised platform, attired in white satin, with the habitual turban of fringed satin of the same shade twined about her head . . . the gown cut *décolleté.*" Many present noted that Dolley's shoulders and arms were beautiful even at eighty-two. The staid President wrote in his diary, "Towards the close of the evening I passed through the crowded rooms with the venerable Mrs. Madison on my arm."

Returning home to Nashville by a roundabout way, Polk was exhausted by the processions and receptions held everywhere in his honor. The rich French dishes served him in New Orleans upset his stomach so much that he noted, "As soon as an opportunity offered, I asked a servant in a low tone if he could give me a piece of corn bread and boiled ham." One sympathizes with President Polk in his desire for simple, wholesome American food. Lady Bird Johnson's family ran into similar difficulties with Réné Verdon, former French chef at the White House.

After New Orleans, the Polks cancelled further engagements and hurried home, where shortly afterward, on June 15, 1849, James K. Polk died, worn out at fifty-three.

Dolley Madison died just a month afterward, President Zachary Taylor attending her funeral services, which could not have been bettered by those given for a Chief Executive.

Sarah lived on at Polk Place, surrounded by the mementos of her days in the White House. As the most respected woman in Tennessee, the entire state legislature in a body would pay its respects to her each New Year's Day. When the Nashville Guards marched past she would review them from the front steps.

"Margaret, keep your powder dry." This was the daily admonition given Maryland-born Margaret Mackall Smith Taylor by her husband, General Zachary Taylor, when they were on the march. For twenty years in covered wagons she had accompanied him on his arduous journeying from fort to fort. She was truly a soldier's wife, sharing all his hardships while traveling through Indian-infested territory, making brief homes for him in log cabins and tents.

Following the Seminole Wars they moved to Baton Rouge, where at last Margaret had a real home of her own—a galleried cottage that in the early days of Louisiana had belonged to the Spanish commandant.

There in her garden by the Mississippi she waited while Zachary was away gaining new laurels in the Mexican War, where he commanded the American forces. The public interest in Taylor's victories at Palo Alto, Resaca de la Palma, Monterey, and Buena Vista made him a public hero and resulted in "Old Rough and Ready," as he was called, being nominated for President.

Margaret was most unhappy. She was now almost an invalid and considered that, at sixty-four, Zachary had already done enough for his country. She was sure that the further burden of the Presidency would kill him.

The reason attributed to Zachary's neglecting to answer the Whigs' letter notifying him in Baton Rouge of his nomination for the Presidency was its arrival marked "postage due." Zachary refused to accept unpaid mail. At that time, the Post Office carried "collect letters" which could be sent without postage prepayment.

Upon winning the Presidency, Zachary told audiences on his way to Washington that Margaret "had made a nightly prayer for several months that Henry Clay might be elected President in his place."

Finally Margaret set out with a heavy heart for the White House, where she cloistered herself in her own suite, nostalgically furnished to resemble her beloved cottage in Baton Rouge. While Washington gossiped because she refused to play an active role as First Lady, saying that her family were forced to hide her because she smoked a corncob pipe—which was untrue—her twenty-two-year-old daughter, pretty Mrs. Betty Bliss, performed her mother's duties as official hostess.

Zachary's favorite horse, Whitey, that had carried him

into battle during the Mexican War, was given the freedom of the White House lawn. The President enjoyed "strolling over the lawn among the company, ready to shake hands with anyone who chose to introduce himself."

Fifty years later Zachary's letters were published with the following foreword:

"Many absurb and cruel stories were printed about Mrs. Taylor's character, habits, and daily life, passed up by her descendants with silent contempt, and perhaps for that reason accepted as true, in part at least, by the public."

An eyewitness account was written by Mrs. (Varina Howell) Jefferson Davis. (Incidentally, her predecessor, Sarah Knox Taylor, was the Taylors' second daughter, who died of typhoid fever three months after her wedding to the man who would one day become first President of the Confederacy.) This account gives a true and valuable picture of Margaret Taylor while she was living in the White House:

"I always found the most pleasant part of my visit to the White House to be passed in Mrs. Taylor's bright pretty room where the invalid, full of interest in the passing show in which she had not the strength to take her part, talked most agreeably and kindly to the many friends admitted to her presence. She always appeared at the family dinners to which a few friends were unceremoniously bidden, of which many charming ones were given during General Taylor's administration, and ably bore her share in the conversation at the table.

"The President at one of these dinners at which I was present, after telling an anecdote of his Army life in which his wife had taken part, turned to Jefferson Davis and said, 'You know my wife was as much of a soldier as I was.' His every look and tone bespoke respect, esteem, and love."

But Margaret Taylor was a prophetess. Her husband's sojourn in the White House was short, for some sixteen months later, after attending an Independence Day celebration at the site of the Washington Monument, he returned to the White House where he "feasted on cherries and iced milk against the protestations of Dr. Wotherspoon, who was his guest," and "soon afterward he was seized with a violent attack of cholera Morbus." He died July 9, 1850.

Mrs. Jefferson Davis leaves a word picture of the effect it had upon the grieving Margaret:

"When General Taylor died, I saw her endure all the torture of a state funeral. Mrs. Taylor was worn to a shadow, and lay without uttering a sound, but trembled silently from head to foot as one band after another blared the funeral march of the different organizations, and the heavy guns boomed in quick succession to announce the final parting."

Margaret lived on for two more years and then was laid to rest beside her warrior husband in Springfield, Kentucky.

There was little happiness in the White House for Mary Todd Lincoln, most tragic of all First Ladies. When her young son Willie died she never again went into his room. Flowers were banned from the White House because he had loved them.

Criticized on every side, Mrs. Lincoln confessed to young Mary Harlan: "You should go out every day and enjoy yourself—trouble comes soon enough, my dear child. . . . I know full well by experience, power and high position do not ensure a bed of roses."

During the War Between the States she was verbally crucified in the press. Being a Southerner, even her loyalty to her husband, the President, and the nation was questioned. Three of her half-brothers died in action. The assassination of Lincoln was a blow from which she never seemed to recover. She was too ill to attend his funeral, lying upstairs in a darkened room, while below souvenir hunters ravaged the White House. "The rabble ranged through it at will," wrote Mary Clemmer Ames. "Silver and dining ware were carried off and have never been recovered."

To pay her debts the former First Lady attempted to sell her dresses on New York's Broadway. Assailed in the newspapers for this unprecedented action she cried, "If I had committed murder in every State in this blessed Union, I could not be more traduced. An ungrateful country this."

Wandering in self-imposed exile, Mary Todd Lincoln returned to America upon the *Amérique* in October 1888. In deep mourning, her once-lovely chestnut hair streaked with white, she was pushed into the crowd by a policeman to enable Sarah Bernhardt, the actress, to pass by in her carriage.

First Ladies Eliza McCardle Johnson and Lady Bird Johnson have several similarities, for not only did their Vice President husbands become President upon the assassination of their predecessors, but both were Southern born and both married Johnsons.

President Andrew Johnson, a former tailor, followed President Abraham Lincoln in the White House. A poor tailor, he had first met Eliza McCardle, a shoemaker's daughter, in the Tennessee mountain village of Greenville. She taught him to write; he had already learned by himself how to read.

Eliza fostered his interest in politics, clipped speeches from newspapers and magazines for him to read and study, and later, when he served terms in the state legislature and Congress, stayed behind in Greenville supervising the property interests they had thriftily acquired.

When Lincoln appointed Johnson as Military Governor

of Tennessee, the family were ostracized by their Confederate neighbors. Later, Eliza's home was confiscated for use as a Confederate barracks and hospital. Her son-in-law, Colonel Daniel Stover, was head of a saboteur organization known as "The Bridge Burners." Both his wife, Mary Johnson Stover, and Eliza would leave food for him on the mountains, where such rugged life broke his health, causing his death at thirty-five.

Eliza was fifty-eight years old when Andrew became President. Suffering from tuberculosis and the privations of war, she was already a confirmed invalid. She chose a small bedroom in the northwest corner of the White House, and there she spent her days. Unlike Margaret Taylor she was not unhappy, for her entire family were around her: her sons, Robert, who acted as his father's secretary, and Andrew, Jr., still at school in Georgetown; her daughter Martha Johnson Patterson and husband, Senator David Trotter Patterson of Tennessee, and their two children; and the widowed Mary Johnson Stover, "a dignified statuesque blonde, with a few very fine points which a fashionable butterfly once said would make any woman a belle if she knew how to make the best of them." The Johnson girls were noted for their modesty in wearing high-necked gowns when fashion decreed bare necks and shoulders.

While Martha acted as official hostess, Eliza spent her days advising her husband when he was troubled or reading, sewing, and playing with her grandchildren.

Martha's contribution during their tenure of the White House was not unlike that of Jacqueline Kennedy in our own era—the refurbishing of the Executive Mansion, which was suffering from the effects of wartime overuse and vandalism. Mary Clemmer Ames records:

"The family of the new President arrived in June. The house looked anything but inviting. Soldiers had wandered unchallenged through the entire suites of parlors. The East

Room, dirty and soiled, was filled with vermin. Guards had slept upon the sofas and carpets till they were ruined, and the immense crowds who, during the preceding years of war, filled the President's house continually had worn out the already ancient furniture. To put aside all ceremony and work incessantly was the portion of Mrs. Patterson from the beginning. It was her practice to rise very early, don a calico dress and spotless apron, and then descend to skim the milk and attend the dairy before breakfast."

Martha not only scrubbed floors but milked Eliza's two Jersey cows. In the afternoon she was dressed to receive official callers.

When Congress appropriated $30,000 to renovate the White House, Martha found it would take this amount alone to repair and furnish the parlors. By "making over" and sheer industry, the White House interior was so improved that with the exception of the East Room it was used for the New Year's reception of 1867.

Andrew and Eliza were the first President and First Lady officially to welcome a Queen. She was Queen Emma, widow of King Kamehameha IV of Hawaii, then the Sandwich Islands, who sailed from England on the Cunard ship *Java*, arriving in New York City August 8, 1866. She was received by President Johnson, who introduced his family to her on August 14, 1866.

Andrew Johnson's attempt to carry out Lincoln's liberal policies of reconstruction and reconciliation brought him into bitter conflict with the Radical Republicans. The Tenure of Office Act of March 2, 1867, prohibited the President from removing a cabinet officer without Senate approval. On August 12, 1867, in defiance of this act, President Johnson dismissed a cabinet officer, Secretary of War, Edwin McMasters Stanton, a Radical Republican. The President appointed General of the Army Ulysses Simpson Grant to act *ad interim*.

The Senate, declaring Stanton's removal illegal, ordered his reinstatement. Grant returned to his Army duties while Stanton again headed the War Department.

On February 21, 1868, President Johnson replaced Stanton with Brevet-Major-General Lorenzo Thomas, to whom he wrote: "You are hereby authorized and empowered to act as Secretary of War *ad interim*, and will immediately enter upon the discharge of the duties pertaining to that office."

Impeachment proceedings were instituted against President Johnson by the House of Representatives, February 24, 1868, with the following resolution: "Resolved: that Andrew Johnson be impeached of high crimes and misdemeanors." The charges brought against him were usurpation of the law, corrupt use of the veto power, interference at elections, and misdemeanors.

The impeachment proceedings were held from March 13 to May 26, 1868, with Chief Justice Salmon Portland Chase of the United States presiding in the Senate Chambers.

Associate Justice Samuel Nelson of the Supreme Court administered the following oath to the Chief Justice: "I do solemnly swear that in all things appertaining to the trial of the impeachment of Andrew Johnson, President of the United States, now pending, I will do impartial justice according to the Constitution and laws. So help me God."

This oath was then administered by the Chief Justice to fifty-four Senate members.

Thirty-five Senators voted for conviction, nineteen for acquittal. As a two-thirds vote was necessary for conviction, Johnson was acquitted by one vote.

Throughout all the strain of the trial, Eliza McCardle Johnson had remained calm and cheerful. When a messenger brought the glad news of Andrew's acquittal, she joyfully exclaimed, "I knew he'd be acquitted; I knew it!"

The two wives of President Woodrow Wilson contributed each in her own way to the taxing role of First Lady.

To marry Wilson, Georgia-born Ellen Louise Axson Wilson forgot her own ambitions to be a painter. The day before her father's inauguration, their youngest daughter, Eleanor Randolph Wilson, lay on the floor crying, "It will kill them—it will kill them both."

President William Howard Taft, the outgoing incumbent of the White House, told them, "I'm glad to be going—this is the lonesomest place in the world." However, once the Wilsons moved in they enjoyed it.

"Isn't it lovely, children?" said Mrs. Wilson to her three daughters as they gazed at the Washington Monument from a south window. A large Victrola was among their family furnishings.

Mother and daughters worshiped Wilson. "They pampered him and petted him and looked up to him as their lord and master," observed Ike Hoover, White House Chief Usher.

When Wilson became the first Chief Executive to address Congress in person since President John Adams, Ellen Wilson told him, "That's the sort of thing Roosevelt would have loved to do, if he had thought of it."

"Yes, I think I have put one over on Teddy," her husband wryly replied.

Two of their daughters wed in the White House. Jessie married Francis Bowes Sayre on November 25, 1913, in the East Room, and Eleanor, William Gibbs McAdoo on May 7, 1914, in the Blue Room.

Ellen made a rose garden and also lined the path to her husband's office with roses. No one outside the family realized how ill she was. Some days she could only watch the gardeners from a chair.

Like Lady Bird Johnson, she had a civic desire close to her heart: to replace the slums that marred much of Washington's beauty. Just before she died, August 6, 1914, Ellen whispered to her husband that she would be happy if she knew the Tenement Bill had passed. Congress gave the assurance that it would.

The President himself arranged her body upon a couch and then sat by it for two nights. . . .

On December 10, 1915, Wilson married a comely widow, Mrs. Norman (Edith Bolling) Galt, at her modest home on Twentieth Street, Washington. Chief White House Usher Ike Hoover arranged the background of maidenhair fern; the dark-eyed bride wore a black picture hat and an afternoon gown with long pointed sleeves.

During their controversial courtship the happy pair had met secretly at 12 West Tenth Street, New York City, for Thanksgiving, at which time the back and front staircases of the old red brick mansion (where Etiquette Authority Emily Post had spent her childhood and where pioneer woman fresco painter Isabel Lydia Whitney lived for twenty-five years) were festooned with Secret Service men instead of the traditional decorations.

A minor catastrophe occurred during the meal, for the aged butler was unable to find the gravy bowl and, much to his chagrin, was reduced to using an oatmeal bowl. The table upon which they ate is now preserved in the dining room of the Dr. Joseph Johnson House, Charleston, South Carolina, the house-museum commemorating Isabel Lydia Whitney.

To the White House came Edith's sewing machine . . . while her husband whistled "Oh, You Beautiful Doll" many times during their honeymoon. He was also adept at doing impersonations, the cakewalk, and a jig.

During the time the Americans fought in World War I, Edith kept a flock of sheep on the White House lawns, their wool realizing $100,000 for the Red Cross.

Christening United States merchant vessels, she gave them Indian names in honor of her ancestress, Princess Pocohontas of Virginia, where she too was born.

Ellen accompanied the President on a triumphal tour of Europe, during which they dined from an all-gold table service with King George V and Queen Mary at Buckingham Palace. Later, while traveling from Washington to the West Coast to promote the League of Nations which Wilson passionately favored, the President collapsed and had to return to Washington. His several ailments included paralysis of the left side.

For seventeen months the First Lady and Dr. Cary T. Grayson took care of the invalid. While it was widely rumored that they were running the country, others insisted Edith ran it alone. One correspondent referred to this period as "the Mrs. Wilson regency." Modestly she called it "my stewardship."

Wilson lived out his days as President, not dying until February 3, 1924. Edith found solace in the knowledge that he was the only President to be buried in the National Cathedral at Washington.

She visited Poland in 1931 to unveil his statue given by an old friend, Ignace Jan Paderewski, the musician and statesman. Until her own death in 1962 she remained a revered figure in the Washington scene.

~ 13 ~

A Working First Lady

* *

BOTH Lyndon and Lady Bird have always shown great respect and veneration for old age. "I get my advice from old men, my action from the young," Lyndon once said. So in April 1964 Lady Bird was dispatched to Cleveland's Riverview Golden Age Center to discuss the President's federal health and housing plans, her job being to give a direct report to the President. It was a task that a homemaker like Lady Bird fully enjoyed. After all, it is no good sending a woman to inspect housing projects for the elderly if she doesn't know how to cook!

This visit to Cleveland included a vital, timely speech made April 20 before the delegates to the YWCA National Convention. "When we have traveled on assignments abroad—to Greece, Turkey, the Philippines—the letters Y-W-C-A are a common tongue and they seem to say— 'This is an outpost of democracy,'" she began, then, touching on women's desires in today's world, continued:

"We want stable conditions for a home life free of unemployment. The biggest crippler of family life is the inability to get a job. People don't want handouts. They don't want doles. They want to learn the skills they can exchange for a paycheck.

"We want a good home environment for our children. And, if we mean this and strive for it effectively, it encompasses a really massive attack on the part of city dwellers to demand long-range, imaginative efforts to make our cities clean, functional, and beautiful."

The journey home from Cleveland to Washington proved an adventure for her and a headache for Lyndon. An electric storm was so unnerving aboard the United Airlines Viscount on which she had flown to Cleveland that she decided to drive back. This trip proved no picnic either, for heavy rain and fog made driving hazardous during the nine-hour journey. She stopped for dinner at a Howard Johnson restaurant, phoning her anxious husband at the White House. As the restaurant had been informed in advance of Mrs. Johnson's pending arrival, a table had been set up in readiness for her party. The waitress was so uneasy that she made a real butterfingers of herself. Afterward she confessed, "I was so nervous having to serve the boss's wife!"

Back on the road, her borrowed Cadillac developed mechanical trouble. At a service garage the First Lady remained seated while three mechanics discovered the fuel filter to be blocked. They had a new one installed in only five minutes.

Having left Cleveland at 4:29 P.M., the agents driving declared that speed limits of 65 to 70 miles an hour on the slippery turnpikes would be upheld. At 1:23 next morning they drove up to the White House, where a welcoming light still burned in the President's office.

On March 11, 1964, the First Lady left upon an official journey to Greece with former President Harry S. Truman, where they represented the United States at the state funeral of King Paul. Lady Bird had happy memories of his friendly widow, Queen Frederika, so she was an appropriate choice.

With national feeling running high over strife-torn Cyprus, Lady Bird and Truman arrived to be greeted with such signs as "Truman Go Home" and "America, hands off Cyprus." (Prince Philip, a former Greek prince and husband of the Queen of England, who two days previously had presented him with a third son, expected to find similar demonstrations, but fortunately they did not materialize.) The pomp and pageantry of the Greek Orthodox funeral provided good material for Lady Bird's diary. . . .

On Tuesday, March 24, 1964, Lady Bird found herself at the Marshall Space Flight Center, Alabama, visiting rockets and relatives. Sixty of the latter appeared from various parts of the state where her own parents had been born in Autauga County. Lynda Bird had breakfasted with Lady Bird in Washington, which meant getting up at 6 A.M. "Lynda being partial to sleeping in the morning, this was quite a tribute," quipped her mother. "Might as well be living on the farm." More than a thousand people gathered at the airport for a glimpse of the First Lady.

Before the rocket demonstration, Lady Bird presided at the head of the luncheon table in the administration building. She was seated between eighty-seven-year-old "Uncle John" Pattillo of Billingsley and Cousin Edwina Mitchell, director of a women's prison at Wetumpka. Later she watched a test firing of the first stage of Saturn I, calling it "fantastic," then after a few seconds' interval she observed, "If the mind of man can do as much with machines as this, surely it can do as much with human engineering for peace."

Because of her interest in the role of women in today's world, Lady Bird asked that women working on the space project, including skilled women technicians, be brought forward to meet her.

Everywhere she went the First Lady, in her bright apricot wool coat, seemed vibrantly alive. Three hundred women from across the state met her at an afternoon reception, where her energy seemed boundless. Finally, after a sixteen-hour-long day, Lady Bird was back home in the White House.

Washington society reporters were well pleased with the sociability of the First Lady and her daughters. From the beginning Lady Bird followed the late Eleanor Roosevelt's pattern of being readily accessible to the press.

When the President sensibly asked an old friend of the family, seasoned newspaper woman Elizabeth Carpenter, to act as his wife's press secretary ("Go and help Lady Bird," he said), he did the First Lady a great service. At one time Mrs. Carpenter ran a Washington news bureau with her husband and was familiar with reporters and the kind of news they are after.

Mrs. Carpenter—or Liz, as she was familiarly known—was as dynamic in her own way as the woman she served so well.

First impressions are often helped by one's surroundings and the same could be said of Mrs. Carpenter. Her office-sitting room at the White House was rich and warm with bright colors like "Christmas all the year round." She was the only woman I ever met since coming to live in America who offered me candy without making a remark about calories or dieting. Her laugh was infectious; she was a pleasant buffer for the First Lady.

Cosmopolitan Mrs. Kennedy, in spite of all the news she made during her short White House tenure, was often remote to the newspaper reporters' needs. She could never be reached directly, while her secretaries had little idea of the kind of human-interest stories journalists craved for their columns. Mrs. Eisenhower employed as her social secretary a lady whom one reporter called "about as helpful as a Secret Service agent." She thought that Mrs. Eisenhower should be *protected* from the press. As for Mrs.

Truman, she always avoided newsmen as if they had the plague.

The first working newspaperwoman to hold the position of press secretary to a First Lady, Mrs. Carpenter saw to it that Mrs. Johnson became a personality in her own right and not just an accessory to the President.

In defining her unique position, Mrs. Carpenter said:

"My job is to help Mrs. Johnson help the President. I have known Mrs. Johnson for twenty years and I can tell you emphatically she is not trying to establish a new identity or a new image or a new sphere of influence or a new anything. She is simply trying to be the best wife she knows how to a husband whose job is President of the United States.

"You've got to understand that her husband's career consists of thirty years on the political ladder. When she married Mr. Johnson he was a secretary to a Congressman, then he became a Congressman himself, then a U.S. Senator, then the Senate Majority Leader, then the Vice President, and now the President. So that their whole adult life, their entire life together, has been spent in government. Mrs. Johnson understands politics. She understands people. She knows all about image-making. There's very little I can contribute in the face of her broad experience and knowledge.

"What I try to do is to see that she gets a good press, because she considers a good press an aid to her husband; that's been her over-all objective in her marriage—to help her husband.

"To get a good press I try being as helpful as I can to the people who cover the family side of the White House. I take phone calls at home at all hours of the night. I make an honest effort to answer every question. I try to earn the respect of my colleagues, because I am one of them. I have a husband who's a newspaperman. I used to cover the Washington beat myself, and I expect to return to that beat. I know what it is to scrounge around for an angle, to follow up on a query. You want a story? My job is to help you get it."

Mrs. Carpenter, a fifth-generation Texan, was born in Salado, Texas, in a twenty-four-room mansion built by her grandfather. While a student at Austin High she edited *The Maroon*, the school newspaper, where she met her future husband, Leslie Carpenter, the paper's business manager. They later attended the University of Texas, both majoring in journalism.

Graduating in 1942, Mrs. Carpenter went to Washington—her graduation gift—where she called at the office of her Congressman, Representative Lyndon B. Johnson, who was away fighting at the time in the Pacific. In his place she met Lady Bird who, Mrs. Carpenter says, was "running his office and seemingly running it very well."

Getting a job at $25 a week with Esther Van Wagoner Tufty's news bureau as a secretary-reporter, she was to marry Leslie Carpenter, then a Navy ensign, in the National Cathedral. After World War II ended they opened their own news bureau. Mrs. Carpenter gave birth to two children, a son, Scott, nineteen, and a daughter, Christy, now sixteen.

Over the years the Johnsons and Carpenters became good family friends. Mrs. Johnson and Mrs. Carpenter's relationship is based on mutual trust and admiration of each other's capabilities.

Leslie Carpenter has described his wife as "a wonderful wife and mother . . . everything a man could ask for." "There's only one thing," he confessed, "that Liz needs to make her completely happy, and no one—not even Mrs. Johnson who loves her very much—can provide it. As Liz puts it, 'One day in my life I would like to be thin.' "

When Lady Bird returned to her native South on May 11, 1964, she called upon it to grasp its birthright of tomorrow, "strong in its fairness and mighty in its contributions," declaring, "The South is on the march, moving resolutely toward the future. No frontier in all the world is more truly open than the frontier of the South. It is an old, old region—but it is a new and dynamically going-forward region, too, where the best of the past can be merged alike with the finest of the present and with the highest hopes of the future."

She was speaking at the Emory University Honors' Day Convocation in Atlanta, Georgia. Earlier she had dedicated a $10,000,000 auditorium at the United States Communicable Diseases Center, at which time she was hard put to thrust her beribboned spade into the sunbaked clay. As she left the Center she was handed an envelope by ten-year-old John Taylor of nearby Decator addressed to the President. Inside was a photograph of John playing the piano to his pet beagle. "This is the way I entertain my beagle," read the accompanying note. Mrs. Johnson promised personally to deliver the letter to her husband.

Lady Bird had arrived in Atlanta upon the same commercial airliner as one of its most famous and controversial residents, Dr. Martin Luther King, Jr., the civil rights leader, whom she went personally to greet.

A few days later the First Lady was the center of some unpleasantness at the hands of two Republican Congressmen who saw fit to travel hundreds of miles south to Alabama to "investigate" the living conditions of Mrs. Johnson's tenants. Judging by irate editorials appearing in newspapers across the country, their detective work proved more of an embarrassment to them than to the First Lady.

Congressman David Martin of Nebraska and Congressman Gene Snyder of Kentucky, complete with tape recorders, arrived in Autauga County where Lady Bird owns some 3,000 acres of land inherited from her family. Once run-down cotton-producing country, Lady Bird turned it over to timber. However, she hadn't the heart to dispossess several elderly folk who had lived there all their lives. They had pleaded to be allowed to stay on in their own homes.

Reported the visiting Congressmen, "We were shocked at the squalor we found."

Replied pleasant-faced Mrs. Willie Cutler (they give girls boys' names in the South), wife of seventy-five-year-old Charles Cutler: "We have lived here for fifty years. . . . We like it. I want to stay here until the Good Lord takes me away."

Explained Elizabeth Carpenter: "Most of the families are very elderly and have no place to go. They want to stay there. She [Mrs. Johnson] is really making it possible for them to live out their days at five dollars a month, and she sends them boxes of clothes."

Actually the Cutlers received $150 a month in Welfare aid, and paid $5 monthly for their four-roomed house, barn, and four acres of land. As Mrs. Carpenter noted, the First Lady could profitably have turned the land to timber, as she had done the rest. Instead she had given express orders that her family's old tenants should be allowed to remain just as long as they liked. As for the clothing, Charles Cutler proudly displayed three tailor-made suits from the President's Senatorial days, saying, "They make me feel just like I'm a Senator myself."

When told of the President's newly proposed poverty program, Willie declared that if "*he*" was going to run it then "it's sure gonna be a fine thing."

The Congressmen scarcely had time to return to Washington with their tapes and photographs when their tactics met with a barrage of criticism. A *New York World-Telegram and Sun* editorial dated May 18, 1964, is a good example:

"The report of two Republic Congressmen who turned amateur sleuth to investigate conditions on Alabama property owned by Mrs. Lyndon Johnson hardly can be a source of pride to anyone, including the investigators. . . . Their low-level gumshoeing, financed by the House Republican Congressional Committee, was patently political. In that light, their pious charge that President Johnson's war on poverty is 'nothing more than an election year gimmick' rings with all the authenticity of a wooden nickel."

That same month, while visiting the Metropolitan Opera in New York City—the first member of a First Family to do so in nineteen years—Lady Bird discovered that even the First Lady cannot always retain her dignity.

Given a warm applause as she returned to her box for the third act, she was still smiling her acknowledgment when she sat down, promptly disappearing from sight. While the audience gasped, Lady Bird located her misssing chair.

During August, 1964, in an effort to create interest in tourism and conservation, Lady Bird visited the scenic states of Montana, Utah, and Wyoming with Interior Secretary Stewart L. Udall. What the First Lady termed a "land and people tour" lasted four long days, each averaging more than eighteen hours.

The most memorable and relaxing part of her trip was spent sailing leisurely down the Snake River in a 27-foot-long rubber raft. For once completely isolated from official duties, she could simply sit, relax, and admire the scenery. Thrilled by her first glimpse of Wyoming's famous Teton Mountains she exclaimed, "Look, y'all, just look!" Then she spottted a flock of Canadian geese flying in formation. "Aren't they gorgeous," she exclaimed, as she made a note for her diary, "strung out across the sky?"

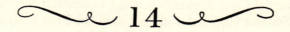

14

Great Victory

* *

WEDNESDAY, August 26, 1964, Atlantic City, New Jersey: this was a night of memories for Lady Bird Johnson. Four years ago she was choking back the tears as she watched her husband's quest for his party's greatest prize fade at a noisy convention. This time it seemed everybody was yelling for her man rather than for someone else.

It was convention time again. Lyndon had been plunged into the Presidency through a terrible tragedy; now was his chance to win the nation's top office in his own right. The Republicans had chosen Senator Barry Goldwater of Arizona as their top candidate.

All eyes seemed to be upon Lady Bird and her daughters that hot summer night. The Johnsons were there as a family: Lynda Bird, who had already demonstrated that in the political field she was truly her father's daughter, and uninhibited Luci, who captured all hearts the afternoon she went wading in the warm Atlantic surf.

With the Presidential nomination going to Lyndon and the Vice Presidential nomination to Minnesota's Hubert Humphrey, Lady Bird knew that once more she would soon strike the campaign trail. She was given—or rather gave herself—perhaps the toughest territory of the entire campaign:

the South, her own birthplace, and now, because of the controversial Civil Rights Bill, solid Goldwater territory.

But Senator Goldwater did not stop the First Lady of the United States or her Lady Bird Special. It was not an easy trip, for at times youthful hecklers not old enough themselves to vote behaved in the manner of similar organized groups found in worldwide trouble spots. Their behavior was both uncivilized and revolting.

On Tuesday, October 7, wearing a bright red suit, Lady Bird was given a warm send-off by the President, who called her "one of the greatest campaigners in America."

Said he, "I'm proud that I'm her husband."

The first stop was Alexandria where, with a smiling Lynda Bird at her side, she praised the South for its headway.

"I think," she declared, "we all understand that the hard duty of assuring equal and constitutional rights to all Americans falls not only on the President of the United States but upon all who love this land. I am sure we will rise to that duty."

The Lady Bird Special sped on to Richmond, Virginia, for more speeches. A large sign cartooned Barry Goldwater as a bespectacled tomcat pouncing on a minute sparrow. FLY AWAY LADY BIRD screamed the caption. This was offset in Charlotte, North Carolina, where three high school bands, to the tune of "Hello Dolly," greeted her with "Hello Lady Bird."

Columbia, South Carolina, was the scene of such a display of heckling and goonery that an incensed Lynda Bird gave those responsible a piece of her mind: "I am sure those few rude shouts and boos are not from the good people of South Carolina—but from the state of confusion."

Governor Donald S. Russell was white with anger. "I am proud to be Governor of South Carolina," he announced, "because South Carolinians are men and women of good manners and hospitality."

Lady Bird replied to her detractors with the quiet dignity

of a true Southern lady. "This is a country of many view-points. I respect your rights to express yours. . . . Now it's my turn to express mine."

The outcome of the disgraceful performance was a telegram sent from Dr. Thomas F. Jones of the University of South Carolina, some of whose students, it had been reported, had been among the participants. Said he: "The entire university community has been shocked and embarrassed at the misconduct that marred your visit. . . . The behavior reported to me is characteristic of barbarians and not the characteristic of educated and cultured adults."

Lady Bird went on to Charleston, called by its inhabitants "The Holy City." There Luci Baines was to have ridden with her mother in an open carriage but a tired throat kept her on the train. Lynda Bird had returned to school because, as Lady Bird explained, "About two days is all she could take away from her studies and still get good grades."

The First Lady obliged photographers, troubled by the strong early morning light, by walking down the center of historic Church Street. At St. Michael's Church on busy Meeting Street she observed that two signers of America's Constitution, General Charles Cotesworth Pinckney and John Rutledge, were buried in the churchyard. She visited the Nathaniel Russell House, headquarters of Historic Charleston Foundation, whose rehabilitation project in what was once the run-down Ansonborough section of the city is the kind of undertaking dear to Lady Bird's heart. There she met the energetic Foundation's director, Frances Smythe Edmunds (Mrs. S. Henry Edmunds).

Women reporters on the Lady Bird Special raved over Charleston's handsome Mayor Palmer Gaillard, dubbing him "the strong movie star type." Lady Bird, clutching hand-colored prints of the Dock Street Theater and St. Philip's Church by local artist Julia Homer Wilson, personally congratulated the Mayor for his knowledge of Charleston's history and his ability as a guide. Her Secret Service men showed an admirable display of patience when a persistent woman pinned Goldwater buttons to their lapels.

One anecdote of the Charleston visit is worth recording because it emphasizes Lady Bird's kindly understanding of the press. When a *Life* photographer broke his tooth she insisted upon being photographed with the dentist, Dr. Stanley Karesh and his family, after the tooth had received an emergency "fixing."

All down the Battery, which she had particularly wanted to see, knowing that Charleston's roots were deep in this historic area, old ladies peeped through wooden lattice blinds, then closed them in her face. It was all very sad. Back on the Lady Bird Special, Lady Bird made the apt comment, "It looked like an exquisite corpse."

Lady Bird's trip might well have ended in tragedy and a repetition of that awful moment in Dallas when a President was killed, for during a 1966 investigation of Ku Klux Klan activities it was disclosed that a Mississippi Klansman had suggested wrecking the Lady Bird Special in order to assassinate the First Lady. Fortunately Lady Bird was spared so ghastly a fate.

Arriving in historic New Orleans, she heard Luci declare to an enthusiastic cosmopolitan audience, "We are going to learn today if we are going to lead tomorrow."

This time Lady Bird may not have won the South, as Bobby Kennedy declared she had once before, for the odds were stacked too unevenly. Nevertheless she soon had the satisfaction of seeing Lyndon elected President by a landslide victory that even exceeded the 60.8 per cent of the vote received by Franklin D. Roosevelt in 1936.

She stood gazing up into her husband's eyes, looking for all the world like a little girl, in her red wool coat and off-the-face velour hat.

Lady Bird held the Johnson family Bible while Lyndon slowly recited the oath of office.

"... So help me God."

It was over; she smiled and caught her breath as he squeezed her arm. This was the proudest moment of her life. How far removed it seemed from that sad swearing-in aboard the plane waiting to take the coffin of another President back to Washington!

But now they must go forward, Lyndon and Lady Bird marching before their Great Society. She wanted so much for Lyndon to become a great President in his own right. "One of the most fascinating human beings ever to become President of the United States," *The London Observer* had called him.

She realized that the cannons across the Potomac were no longer booming and that Lyndon had begun to speak.

My fellow countrymen. . . . We have no promise from God that our greatness will endure. We have been allowed by Him to seek greatness with the sweat of our hands and the strength of our spirit. If we fail now, we shall have forgotten in abundance what we learned in hardship: that democracy rests on faith, that freedom asks more than it gives, and that the judgment of God is harshest on those who are most favored.

If we succeed, it will not be because of what we have but it will be because of what we are; not because of what we own, but rather because of what we believe. For we are a nation of believers. Underneath the clamor of building and the rush of our day's pursuits, we are believers in justice and liberty and union, and in our own Union. We believe that every man must some day be free. And we believe in ourselves.

By coincidence he had chosen to end with a verse from the Second Book of Chronicles, Chapter I, which Dr. Billy Graham, the evangelist, had used earlier that day in Washington's National City Christian Church which the President and his family had attended.

> Give me now wisdom and knowledge, that I may go out and come in before this people; for who can judge this thy people, that is so great?

"There is a spiritual dimension to leadership, which this Administration has already recognized," said Dr. Graham.

Inauguration Day started at 6:40 A.M. for the Johnsons. Outside it was cold and frosty, a typical wintry morning in the capital. The Washington Monument, Lady Bird's favorite view, "because it gives her courage," gazed back like a tower of strength.

They breakfasted together before Lyndon read once more that all-important inaugural address.

With her usual concern for others, Lady Bird wondered if all the relatives had slept well, both in the Executive Mansion and Blair House across the street. Strange how close they made Texas and home seem that wonderful morning.

There were Lyndon's uncle, Huffman Baines; his aunt, Mrs. Joseph Saunders; his brother, Sam Houston Johnson; his sisters, Mrs. Birge Alexander and Mrs. O. P. Bobbitt, with their children, Becky Alexander and Philip Bobbitt; his nephew, Rodney White, and cousin, Ave Johnson Cox.

On Lady Bird's side were her widowed sister-in-law, Mrs. Sarah Taylor, and her daughter Susan; and her brother and sister-in-law, Mr. and Mrs. A. J. Taylor.

"Aunt Jessie," an old family friend and a widow from Texas, had been asked by Lyndon if she was coming to his inauguration.

"I haven't been asked," was her answer.

The Johnsons are not the kind of people to forget old friends. "Pack your dress," ordered Lyndon, putting his arm around the elderly lady, "and come with us. Be at the ranch no later than four-forty. Air Force One won't leave without you."

Another longtime friend, Governor John Connally of Texas, had the unique experience of sleeping in Lincoln's bedroom.

Pennsylvania Avenue is the perfect place for a parade, especially if the weather is kind . . . and it was kind to Lyndon B. Johnson for his inauguration.

Leontyne Price, the Negro prima donna, sang "America the Beautiful"—and the parade was America, composed as it was of people from all walks of life, the rich, the poor, the celebrity, the ordinary man in the street. Each had his part. Everyone seemed oblivious of the bitter cold. Concessionaires did a brisk trade with hot coffee. Hawkers pushed their way in and out through the crowd with Presidential buttons, balloons, and pennants, while from overhead loudspeakers came appropriate music such as "Hello Lyndon" and "We're in the Money."

Everywhere there seemed to be a reporter, a photographer, or a television crew. The happy, jostling crowd appeared totally unaware of the security guards and Secret Service men watching from rooftops as well as the ground. Television scanners and electronic apparatus aided the Secret Service in its gigantic task. Windows on the route had been ordered closed days before.

Time reported, "The Johnsons arrived at the Capitol riding in the same limousine in which Kennedy had been shot, now covered with a new roof of steel and bulletproof glass."

With them was Senator Everett Jordan, of North Carolina, another old friend. Lyndon hurried into a private office in the Rotunda to have his contact lenses inserted. . . . Vinnie Ream's statue of Lincoln looked benignly down—proof that in America boys born in log cabins and lowly farmhouses could still grow up to be Presidents—while a poor postal worker, "a mere slip of a girl" Lincoln had called her, could be lifted to greatness by a benevolent Congress and leave her legacy in marble, as Vinnie Ream had done, as an inspiration for other Presidents who would follow in the footsteps of the Great Emancipator. . . .

Before that American phenomenon, the Inauguration Parade, the President and the First Lady lunched with Congressmen and friends. There was a bouyancy in the air, mingled with excitement and awe.

As they were walking to the luncheon, suddenly the new President turned and kissed Lady Bird on the mouth. For one brief moment her face glowed. Then Lynda Bird drew her father's face toward her and kissed him on both cheeks. Luci kissed him too. Then the Johnsons walked into the future. . . .

The reviewing stand in front of the White House looked formidable with its wall of bulletproof glass.

Because of America's peaceful role in the modern world, no signs of tanks, big guns, or rockets were in evidence. Instead the armed forces were each represented by one division, with token groups from service academies.

With the exception of Texas and Minnesota, which were both allowed an extra band, each state was limited to its Governor's car, one band, a float, and a marching unit.

Various scenes symbolic of Lyndon Johnson's proposed Great Society were portrayed on the floats, including a realistic model of the LBJ Ranch complete with such trimmings as the Pedernales River made from plastic and a tail-wagging beagle!

Everyone loves a parade, and the American public is no exception. In a temperature of 38 degrees, blue noses and numbed legs were forgotten by participants and watchers alike. Even a St. Bernard, mascot of the Chicago Fire Department, carrying a keg of brandy like all good St. Bernards should and appropriately wearing a Texas hat for the occasion, got into the act. When Him, the President's beagle, saw Omar Von Sauliant, the canine strutter, only his leash prevented him from joining the parade.

For a brief, gaudy period the bands and precision marchers took over the Avenue until finally, when the last float had passed the reviewing stand, Lady Bird whispered something in Lyndon's ear.

Quietly he turned and with obvious emotion said: "Thank you very much. You are a wonderful people, and you have made this such a lovely day, and we will try so hard to be worthy of your trust and friendship."

But the long day was far from ended. Five Inaugural balls had been arranged to accommodate the 28,000 invited guests, and, at least for the women, the most rewarding feature of the evening would be a glimpse of the First Lady's inaugural gown.

It was designed by John Moore of New York City (formerly of Alice, Texas); its color was described as "Jonquil yellow," though fellow Texans declared she wore it to honor their own Texas rose.

Lady Bird chose the gown herself from several designs, because she wished to capture "both timelessness and understated elegance." After seeing the finished dress made of double-woven satin and cut on classic lines, she hoped she had "come close to it." In addition she had found yellow "a joyous color" which the President liked to see her wear.

The matching coat gave an illusion of falling from narrow shoulders to a wide hemline. A stand-up collar framed the face, while elbow-length sleeves were circled by wide cuffs of natural sable. She purchased her ensemble through Neiman-Marcus, the Dallas department store she had patronized since girlhood.

Lady Bird's accessories were a single strand of pearls and a pair of diamond and gold earrings given her by the President to mark their thirtieth wedding anniversary. With a becoming upswept coiffure styled especially for the occasion, she looked truly regal.

Twenty-year-old Lynda Bird wore a simple white silk sheath under a matching double-breasted floor-length coat with long sleeves and rhinestone buttons.

Luci's gown was the surprise of the evening, for she had refused to be photographed in advance, explaining she had to study and could not spare the time.

The dress turned out to be rose-petal pink satin with ribbon and shoes to match.

Both Lynda Bird and Luci had problems coping with examinations in addition to all the pre-inaugural functions and activities they were expected to attend. Lynda, then a junior at George Washington University, faced two examinations, while Luci, at the National Cathedral School for Girls, had five! Finally, their schools suggested they take the examinations a week in advance.

The President made the round of all the inaugural balls. There were both memorable and humorous incidents: Lyndon dancing with Lady Bird on an empty floor, hemmed in by an ocean of faces. . . . Luci expertly doing the Watusi, for which she had developed a certain talent. . . . The President helping lift Margaret Truman Daniels over the rail of her box so that he could be her partner for the next dance . . . and at the Sheraton-Park reception his observation that "Never before have so many paid so much to dance so little."

The late Dorothy Kilgallen summed up the whole wonderful day in the January 21 issue of the *New York Journal American:* "Informality was the tone set in advance by the President, who decided that he wasn't going to get into any white tie, tailcoat, and top hat even if he had won the election by the largest landslide ever recorded."

The caption to the photograph accompanying her story added a fitting postscript: "LAST DANCE FOR FIRST LADY. . . . After a long evening and many dance partners, President and Mrs. Johnson share the last dance."

15

She Planted Three Trees

* *

WHEN the First Lady announced that the White House was "looking for Cassatts" to augment its permanent collection, she revealed her deep though rarely publicized interest in paintings.

Mary Cassatt (1844–1926) was the expatriate American of whom Gauguin, comparing her with Berthe Morisot, declared, "Her work has as much charm, but more force." Her paintings had already found favor in the White House, the Kennedys having borrowed two from museums to enjoy in their private dining room.

Lady Bird had happily accepted for the White House Library a two-volume edition of *The American Drawings of John White*, 1577–1590, depicting early Anglo-American history. *The Dictionary of American Biography* describes his work as being "some of the earliest and most valuable of the material for the study of the natural history and aboriginal life in America."

Thanks to Mrs. Johnson's determination, at last a portrait of Eleanor Roosevelt was hung in the White House entrance hall "where," she said, "as many people as possible may see it." This is a happy location, for Mrs. Roosevelt once remarked on a similar occasion when her late husband's statue was placed in an easily accessible London square, "Franklin would have liked it; because he enjoyed having people around him."

The artist, Douglas Chandor, was responsible for the portraits of many world-famous figures, including one of Queen Elizabeth II commissioned by Mrs. Roosevelt to hang in the British Embassy, Washington: President Franklin D. Roosevelt and his World War II ally, the late Sir Winston Churchill.

After Chandor's death in 1953, the portrait of Mrs. Roosevelt remained in the possession of his widow at Weatherford, Texas. Mrs. Johnson felt that it should hang where it belonged, in the White House. Thanks to the White House Historical Association, which sells guidebooks of the Executive Mansion, this was made possible.

It is interesting to note that a pastel of Mrs. Roosevelt, made without her knowledge, hung for many years in her husband's upper office. The President and their children had planned it as a surprise for her fiftieth birthday but she burst into tears at sight of it. A miniature made when she was a little girl hangs in the Roosevelt Library at Hyde Park.

When Mrs. Johnson unveiled the portrait on January 31, 1966, she spoke warmly of the woman who had lived for more than twelve years—longer than any other—in the White House. "When I first looked at Douglas Chandor's portrait of Eleanor Roosevelt, I was struck by the artist's use of Mrs. Roosevelt's hands. They are many hands, busy with all kinds of things, and nothing could be more appropriate. For Eleanor Roosevelt was a woman who had hands for the whole world—fine, strong, sensitive hands that ennobled everything they touched."

Mary Fickett, who played Eleanor Roosevelt in "Sunrise at Campobello," then read from Mrs. Roosevelt's own writings. So, thanks to the First Lady of Beautification, the First Lady of the Busy Hands came home at last!

A New Mexican painter whose work was much admired by the President and First Lady, Peter Hurd, was selected to paint the President's official portrait. The President is shown, book in hand, looking into the future with a view of the city of Washington behind him. It is somewhat reminiscent of the young Lyndon B. Johnson whose photograph as a dedicated youth leader is in his mother's family album.

Explained Hurd: "Know how I found out I had the job? . . . My wife and I were invited to a White House bash for the President of South Korea. I got out my evening clothes, and they smelled of mothballs because we don't use them down here on the ranch. I felt self-conscious as I stood by the President, and then he calmly dropped his bomb when he introduced me to the Korean President. 'I want you to meet the man who's going to do my portrait.'"

While they waited for Hurd to complete the painting, the Johnsons borrowed two of his works done in the 1930s to hang in the White House. "O Pioneers," a tranquil family scene, came from the Smithsonian Institution and was hung in the foyer leading to the President's office. The other, called "West Bound Mail Stage," shows a stagecoach bumping over rocky terrain as it passes a group of ox-drawn wagons. It was discovered in a storage room at Fort Washington, Maryland, where it had lain forgotten for more than twenty-five years. Nash Castro, Eastern Regional Director of the National Park Service which has supervision of Fort Washington, who found the picture, knew of the Johnsons' interest in the works of Peter Hurd, so he informed the White House. The First Lady said she would be pleased to borrow it for the White House collection. She often enjoyed pausing to look at these works, done, she recalled, during the Roosevelt Administration when Lyndon was a young representative from Texas.

When the President was chosen by *Time* as its "Man of the Year," Hurd did the magazine cover, assisted by his wife Henriette Wyeth, sister of another famous artist, Andrew Wyeth. As a backdrop was the little house in which the President was born, taken from a photograph which proudly hangs in the Johnson family's living quarters at the White House.

Future generations may well recall Lady Bird Johnson as the First Lady who had a love affair with America. President Theodore Roosevelt is remembered as the Conservation President; she could well be named the Conservation First Lady.

Her enthusiasm toward making a more beautiful America is as real as was her predecessor Jacqueline Kennedy's desire to restore the interior of the White House. President Johnson is in complete agreement, declaring when he signed a bill creating an Assateague Island National Seashore: "If future generations are to remember us more with gratitude than with sorrow, we must achieve more than just the miracles of technology. We must leave them a glimpse of the world as God really made it, not just as it looked when we got through with it."

There is much of Lady Bird in his words, the Lady Bird who when she plants a tree is reminded of Thomas Fuller's maxim, "He that plants trees loves others besides himself."

To *Life* she explained her theory: "Marshal Louis Lyautey, the French soldier-statesman, once suggested to his gardener that he plant a tree. The gardener said, 'Why plant it? It won't flower for a hundred years.' The marshal replied, 'In that case, plant it this afternoon.'"

Lady Bird's Aunt Effie first introduced her to the wonders of nature, and she likes to associate the happiest moments of her life with trees and flowers, be it the sweet smell of honeysuckle in Virginia or a walk under the shady oaks on the ranch in Texas. Her girls have both inherited this deep love of the beautiful.

"Ugliness—the gray, dreary, unchanging world of deprived neighborhoods—has contributed to riots, mental ill health, and to crime," declared the First Lady before a joint meeting of the American Forestry Association and the National Council of State Garden Clubs in Grand Teton National Park, Wyoming.

"Preserving the attractiveness of a city is a primary economic asset, a way to get payrolls. The city that is beautiful brings a high return on the dollar. . . . The ugly city is the one which will decline and die."

Predicting the passing of the highway beautification bill that later materialized, she continued, "Even though we do not get all the features we want, if we get a measure of them, it will be a step forward." Prophesying "the longest strides in history" in the next decade, Lady Bird insisted they would be made because "Americans are not just talking about beauty. They are acting. . . . There is a great opportunity for some technician to develop paper products that disintegrate in the rain instead of remaining to clutter up roadsides."

The First Lady somewhat wryly admitted that it was hard to promote an intangible thing like beauty on a national scale "because it does not fit into the Gross National Product or tally up in personal income. Yet," she said, "we know that the loss of beauty diminishes our lives, and its presence enriches us—as individuals and as a nation."

Her own interest in the cause of beautification came, she said, from the fact that those things she best remembers "after fifty years of living" are "golden moments I had spent in some lovely spot, working in my garden where I added three trees to make a quadrangle with an apple tree." Then Lady Bird said she would like for her own epitaph simply, SHE PLANTED THREE TREES.

The American Institute of Park Executives gave to the

First Lady the first honorary membership to go to a woman. At last conservationists had found another White House champion.

While the *Chicago Tribune* sedately headlined HER NAME IS CLAUDIA, AND BEAUTY IS HER AIM, Lady Bird was off literally proving her point in distant parts of the nation. The first President's wife in 140 years to visit officially in Peoria, Illinois, Lady Bird arrived full of enthusiasm to dedicate a new $4,500,000 county courthouse and pleasant gardens set in the heart of a $50,000,000 eight-block downtown renewal project.

"A city is not just a collection of stores and homes and shops," she informed her audience. "It is a place for people to live and, hopefully, it is a place where they can live the good life." She then planted a Japanese cherry tree (and when Lady Bird plants a tree, she plants it properly). When someone asked if it would survive the cold Peoria winter, Mrs. Everett Dirksen pronounced, "If Lady Bird planted this tree, it will survive."

The movement for beautification caught on, not just with the older citizens but among the young as well.

TEN THOUSAND GIRL SCOUTS OF KICKAPOO COUNCIL SALUTE YOU PLEDGING THEIR CONTINUED SERVICES IN THE EFFORTS OF THEIR CITY BEAUTIFUL was typical of the hundreds of messages the First Lady was now receiving.

On Washington's Mall, upon hands and knees, she planted pansies while Secretary of the Interior Stewart L. Udall gave her moral encouragement from a park bench. When Luci saw a picture of Lady Bird planting a dogwood on Interstate 95 she exclaimed, "My mother really digs those trees." (Luci once explained to a group of girls attending the American Optometrics Association Conference in Boston, "Mother is for beauty and I'm for eyes." She then emphasized that her mother is "not just an honorary chairman, she really works on the beautification program.")

Half a century earlier, another First Lady, Helen Herron Taft, wife of President William Howard Taft, dreamed of beautifying the nation's capital with cherry trees. As a result of her interest, as a gesture of friendship the city of Tokyo sent the city of Washington three thousand cherry trees. Today these heralds of spring blooming around the Tidal Basin and Potomac Park bring visitors from every state in the Union.

Lady Bird's quest to beautify Washington prompted the Japanese government to give thousands more cherry trees as a renewed symbol of friendship. Japanese Ambassador Ryuji Takeuchi made the announcement when his own wife and Lady Bird planted two blooming cherries at the Tidal Basin, formally opening the 1965 National Cherry Blossom Festival. They used a gold-plated spade to plant the new trees close to the spot where Mrs. Taft and Viscountess Chinda, wife of the then Japanese Ambassador, planted the first gift of cherry trees in the spring of 1912.

Telling the Ambassador that not only would the trees be enjoyed by the tourists but by "those of us who live here," Lady Bird expressed everybody's thanks with "I do want you to know how very thrilled and delighted everybody is."

On Thanksgiving Night, 1965, the First Lady narrated and appeared in a television movie entitled "A Visit to Washington" which won critical acclaim from the press. The actual filming had been done earlier, during which time Mrs. Johnson earned the respect of the A.B.C. crew for her total cooperation and enthusiasm. Responsible for the filming were John Secondari and his wife, Helen Jean Rogers, award-winning producers of the "Saga of Western Man" series and the "I, Leonardo" show.

One writer described it as "the most exquisite film ever shown of the Nation's Capital." Mrs. Johnson displayed the rare gift of drawing her nationwide audience right into the picture. Not once did she dominate the scene. Instead, Washington was the star.

She pointed out that 70 per cent of the American people live on 1 per cent of its land, and that by A.D. 2000, because of the farm-to-city trend, 90 per cent will then be living on that 1 per cent.

When the filming was completed, the First Lady gave a party for the producers and crew, showing them some color films she had made of Washington's cherry-blossom time; of The Hermitage, Andrew and Rachel Jackson's home at Nashville, Tennessee; of the inauguration of Franklin D. Roosevelt; and of Mount Vernon, which by the time she became First Lady Mrs. Johnson had already visited on eighty-seven occasions—including once in a raging snowstorm.

The A.B.C. crew were amazed at their quality, for she had never disclosed during the filming of their own picture on Washington that she knew the slightest thing about movie making!

Lady Bird's aversion to highway-adjoining junkyards is shared by many of her fellow citizens. Said A.P.'s Jack Bell before the passing of the highway beautification bill: "Never underestimate the power of a woman—especially if she is the wife of the President of the United States. If President Johnson gets his highway bill passed by Congress in the current session, most of the credit will go to Lady Bird Johnson."

As Bell explained, although most projects in Mrs. Johnson's drive to make America beautiful won applause and cooperation, the highway matter was somewhat complicated for it involved nearly all state governors, many of whom preferred the building of more utilitarian farm-to-market roads than scenic highways as proposed in the original version of the legislation President Johnson sent to

Congress. A "billboard lobby" vigorously opposed the removal of signs from sections of primary and interstate highways, while the "junkyard lobby" was vehemently against the screening or removal of junkyards that bordered them.

When on October 22, 1965, the historic Highway Beautification Bill was signed into law, the President gave his wife the first pen, declaring, "As long as I am President, what has been divinely given by nature will not be recklessly taken away by man."

It was his first White House appearance since his gallbladder surgery of some weeks before.

On the previous day, while returning from the hospital, he had noticed that "the maple trees were scarlet and gold." It was then that he told Lady Bird they should make the bill-signing an elaborate ceremony. Telegrams were hurriedly sent to people who had been instrumental in helping with its passage, including several newspaper editors.

Lady Bird seemed to glow as she moved in and out of the assembled crowd. When the President made his speech, he looked constantly at Lady Bird.

"How," asked Lyndon, "do you put a value on the view of the night that is caught in a boy's eyes while he's stretched out in thick grass, watching the million stars that are never seen in our crowded cities, breathing pure, fresh air while in his ears are the sounds of the night, the birds, the crickets, the wind. . . ."

"Our energetic and talented First Lady has opened a new door in the dream of total conservation," applauded the National Wildlife Federation and the Sears-Roebuck Foundation, as they presented her with the first annual Whooping Crane Award for "inspiration and leadership . . . enthusiastic and dedicated effort and distinguished service to conservation."

On February 23, 1966, the First Lady made her longest

one-day speaking trip to that date when she flew 3,000 miles to bring her message of beautification to the American Road Builders Association, an organization of road contractors and highway officials, meeting in Denver, Colorado. With the snowcapped Rockies as an impressive backdrop, no better site could have been chosen for Lady Bird to plead her favorite cause.

Appealing to the nation's road builders to protect their hometown beauty spots from the havoc of traffic inroads, she pleaded, "Review your plans with all who might be affected. You have done this in working with fish, wildlife, and recreation activities. But this type of relationship should be extended to those who speak for other public interests—the private as well as the official groups. Those who are often your critics can come to understand decisions if they are alerted to your problems and your goals early enough."

Calling America, with its 3.6 million miles of highways, as "the road-buildingest nation on earth," Lady Bird said this meant "nearly a mile of pavement for every square mile of land, and a lot more of this country is going under concrete and asphalt." She continued with the warning:

"In disturbing that much of the turf of this beautiful country we have a special obligation, not only in terms of land use, but also in an aesthetic sense. We are obliged to leave it looking as good, if not better, than the way we found it."

Mrs. Johnson was particularly interested in convincing young Americans that preservation of the unspoiled beauty of the American landscape and of its natural resources would be one of their major tasks in the future.

Attending the opening of the first national youth conference on natural beauty held June 27, 1966, in Washington, Lady Bird was accompanied by the President and their three dogs: Kim, Freckles, and Blanco.

Urging her audience to make beauty "an overriding cause of our time," she told delegates, "you have the ear of the nation, and the nation needs your action."

Not content to rest on her laurels, Lady Bird next turned her attention to a legislative movement devoted to the preservation of historic buildings. She was horrified to learn that almost half of the 12,000 structures listed in the American history survey of the National Park Service had already been destroyed!

"The buildings," she said, "which express our national heritage are not simply interesting. They give a sense of continuity and of heightened reality to our thinking about the whole meaning of the American past."

~ 16 ~

Another Eleanor Roosevelt

* *

MORE and more Lady Bird is being compared to Eleanor Roosevelt, who had a similar listening heart and mind. She acts as a second pair of ears for President Johnson, as Mrs. Roosevelt did for her husband. Modestly Lady Bird says, "I'd like to be as good as she was, but I have no feeling that I am."

"If I had a serious problem, I would take it to Mrs. Johnson, and I know she would listen to me and try to help me solve it," confessed a young Washington matron.

Dedicated to her role as First Lady, as she has always been to that of wife and mother, Lady Bird still finds time for the problems of others.

"She's one woman who listens for a change. . . . She listens more than she talks. That's something new in this town," praised a Washington official.

Having known her a long time, Congressional wives are among the indefatigable Mrs. Johnson's best boosters. "You'll have to look a long way to find a woman as bright as Lady Bird," raved a fellow Texan. "She's so capable, but she never brags about it."

Already she has played an important behind-the-scene

role in her husband's quest to find capable women to fill top government posts. To this end her series of White House luncheons for women have been invaluable. For, as columnist Dorothy McCardle noted, "She can spot a capable woman in a very few words—the other woman's words. And she reports her impressions to the President."

Likewise the First Lady has impressed the guests with her blending of charm and brains. Said a longtime Republican woman: "You know, I may very well vote for Lyndon Johnson this time. His wife is so intelligent. If anybody can, she'll make me switch to the Democratic Party."

"It was just a natural transition to launch Women Doers luncheons when Mrs. Johnson became First Lady," explained Elizabeth Carpenter.

At the beginning the guest lists were compiled from people that Mrs. Johnson knew or had heard about, but White House fan mail from across the land suggested the names of other worthy women. Those invited are from different walks of life and geographical areas. For instance, one luncheon included authoress Katherine Ann Porter, singer Marion Anderson and ballerina Maria Tallchief.

"The first thing we ask when someone suggests a woman to be invited to a luncheon," says Mrs. Carpenter, "is: one, is she articulate? and two, can she stick to seven minutes? We've found that the shortest speeches have sparked the most conversation on the subject. Actually we did try having music played during the luncheons but we found it interfered with the conversation and the women would rather talk."

Arriving at the White House can be a little overwhelming, so first of all the luncheon guests are served a small glass of sherry or orange juice in the yellow Oval Room where once Woodrow Wilson proposed to Edith Galt. Then they are invited to enjoy the view from Harry Truman's balcony before finally being seated in the dining room. Zephyr Wright's good cooking is served on china of a different Administration.

On the day Katherine Anne Porter was a guest, Lynda Bird and her friend Warrie Lynn Smith were expecting to be quizzed at George Washington University on Miss Porter's short story, "Maria Concepcion." When they asked her for an authoritative interpretation of her work, she confessed that "authors are usually accused of more symbolism than they put in."

Traveling abroad when Lyndon was Vice President, Lady Bird surprised embassy protocol personnel by requesting meetings with women active in their country's affairs. In the new African nations they visited, Lady Bird and her daughters were a great success, especially in demonstrating American arts and crafts to the inhabitants.

The President was honest when he promised to advance women's status during his Administration, for he has seen first hand the respect and standing his own wife has gained in the world of both business and politics.

Relaxation comes hard for Lady Bird when she is in Washington. One of the few places she finds it is at her hairdresser's.

"Mrs. Johnson said to tell all of you that this is off the record," announced the President one day to waiting photographers. "She is on the way to the beauty parlor."

One of her hairdressers, Jean Louis, of Haute Coiffure Française, admitted he goes to the White House often to comb the First Lady's hair. The other is Per of Georgetown.

Jean Louis discourages any questions about Mrs. Johnson or any special notice being made of her visits to his salon, although others sharing his services at the same time can not fail to notice one Secret Service man standing just inside the entrance or another sitting outside the door of her private room, a telephone placed conveniently at his elbow.

Because of the proprietor's desire to allow the First Lady to retain her privacy, she seems treated almost with indifference, but other clients naturally place themselves in the best position to see Mrs. Johnson when she leaves.

Of course, Lady Bird has had her fair share of detractors, as her predecessor Jacqueline Kennedy did before tragedy made such criticism tasteless. Nevertheless, Mrs. Kennedy was idolized around the world, especially in Europe, as America's most dazzling First Lady. Anyone fated to follow her was certain to suffer by comparison.

First there was the name "Lady Bird," which the First Lady likes to be called. Even in Britain, where lady birds are looked upon as being among the prettiest and most delicate little creatures, a B.B.C. executive who should have known better complained, "She's so *beige!*"

Malcolm Muggeridge, who is always criticizing the British Royal Family, gave them a rest to complain, "Who ever heard of a country with a First Lady named Lady Bird?"

"She looks like every well-dressed woman of means," decided Maggie Daly, *Chicago American* columnist. "She does not have any special flair."

"Lady Bird is a sort of person *qui ne provoque pas les sentiments*—she does not evoke feelings," complained Françoise Giroud, co-editor of Paris's *L'Express* somewhat tediously. "Who cares about a gray lady bird?"

How little Françoise knew the real, live Lady Bird! Perhaps the picture of a fifty-one-year-old woman still in love with her husband and he equally in love with her was too much for the Gallic mind; the one enduring quality of the Johnsons that can be divorced from both the Presidency and politics is their genuine, extrovert love for each other.

Her brother Tony noted that "Lady Bird has been in public life and in the public eye so long that she had learned to be circumspect, even when she's in a situation where she can let hair down."

"I've never talked to anyone who didn't like her," says Blanche Halleck, wife of the House Republican Leader. Lindy Boggs, wife of Louisiana Democratic Congressman Hale Boggs, admits: "I make her sound like a combination of Elsie Dinsmore and the little Colonel . . . but this is the problem with Bird. When you talk about her, you make her sound too good to be true."

In spite of the quotation from Nicole Alphand, wife of the former French Ambassador to the United States, "I suppose that now we will all have to learn to do zee bar-bee-cue," nobody found it a necessity.

White House visitors are pleasantly surprised when the President bursts unceremoniously into one of Lady Bird's tea parties, kisses her on the forehead, and announces, "I love you." They would be more surprised to see the middle-aged couple walk hand in hand of a summer's night in the White House garden, then find a pleasant spot under one of the trees where they can talk quietly together.

The Johnsons' informal news conferences when they walk with the reporters and their beagles please both press and tourists. Lady Bird sometimes finds it hard to keep her place by Lyndon and trails behind, talking to woman reporters. Then when he takes a notion the President makes for the fence, shaking hands through the rails.

One family identified itself as coming from Falfurrias, Texas, which was all that the President needed to hear.

"You all know Mr. Percy Hunter down there?" he asked, his cheeks creasing into a big smile.

"Yes," one of them answered.

"Well, tell him hello for me."

Then the President remembered that the reporters were

still with him, so turning to them, he explained, "That's where they have that good creamery butter."

Nodding her head, Lady Bird agreed. "They have the best creamery butter in the world down there."

Although First Lady in the land, in some ways Lady Bird Johnson has not changed. She still gets stage fright every time she makes a speech.

Returning to her old school town, Marshall, Texas, to address a service club, she recalled her girlish fears of getting top grades and having to make the commencement speech. "But I was saved," she said, a look of obvious relief lighting up her face. "I came in third."

Later, to old Marshall friends, she declared, "Here I am, ten thousand barbecues and several hundred speeches later, and I am still scared."

Actually Lady Bird speaks very well indeed, getting her message across by just being natural, for her warmth and outgoing quality are catching. She insists that "in the space age, passive citizenship is a luxury no one can afford."

Yet, when there is need to be, the First Lady can be both determined and courageous. As wife of the Vice President she was honorary sponsor of a cause marking the fifteenth anniversary of Israel's independence. When an Arab diplomat protested, Lady Bird replied simply that the easiest course for the wife of a public official "would be, of course, never to lend name, hand, or heart to any endeavour, charitable or commemorative.

"I have," she continued, "for whatever small value it may be, tried to be as accessible and available to as many as possible without distinction as to religion, race, or region and certainly including all states of the Middle East. I shall continue to do so."

This substantiates the fact that she is very much the woman of spirit even if many of the stories printed about her during Lyndon's Vice Presidency made her out to be dull and colorless. Said she, "They made me feel like putting on red tights and running down Pennsylvania Avenue."

In spite of having so forceful and demanding a husband, Lady Bird has never lost her own individuality. Neither has she ever tried to "make him over" to her own tastes. She enjoys good literature, plays, and movies; these are not Lyndon's idea of relaxation, so she has never pressed him to conform as many wives would.

Some of Lyndon's surprises would present more than a challenge to the most efficient of First Ladies. There was, for instance, one morning close to Christmas when he rushed into her room with the suggestion, "Bird, let's ask Congress over this afternoon."

Congress came, several hundred of them!

Epilogue

*

IT WAS Lady Bird the mother who flew down to Alabama on February 25, 1966, to speak to the University of Alabama and the American Association of University Women in Tuscaloosa.

"Coming home is always a nostalgic experience, and Alabama is second home to me," she said. All at once there came back to her those happy migrations with Aunt Effie from Texas to the Pattillo family's home.

It was good to be back in her native South.

Before the year was out her younger child would be married and she would be gaining a son. She felt happy as she stood before a large gathering of women, many of whom were students like her own Lynda Bird and Luci. Lady Bird wanted so much to leave them a good message, at the same time explaining what "The Great Society" really means.

She was thinking, too, of her own daughters when she said: "I am speaking particularly to you students, who have before you the wonderful prospect of raising families but also desire to keep current with the world—and to those of you who are facing a new freedom for the first time in your married lives now that the children have flown the coop. I am also speaking to those of you who are active career women already but who seek new dimensions of activity outside your professional duties. . . . Through the centuries, women have been the prodders. Good works go forward in proportion to the number of vital and creative and determined women supporting them. When women get behind a project, things happen."

Then for a few brief moments she was the First Lady leading her audience right through the gates of the Executive Mansion. "Life around the White House these days is very much like what you're doing here. It is one continuing seminar. A short while ago, I was supposed to meet with a group to discuss the women's job corps. We looked around for a place where one hundred women leaders from all over the United States could talk about the hopes and pitfalls of this great venture.

"In the East Room, a ceremony was being held to honor outstanding students from forty states. The Rose Garden couldn't be used because a group of ministers were gathering to discuss community relations. The State Dining Room was being prepared for a luncheon and briefing of businessmen by the President and Cabinet members.

"I didn't dare try for the second floor because Luci and Lynda were in the throes of exams and had issued dramatic pleas to keep everything quiet.

"So we found our meeting place down in a far corner of the South Lawn amid a wonderful grove of trees. Fortunately, it was a sunny day! In one hundred and sixty years, I doubt that this particular part of the White House grounds had been put to such talkative use. But we gathered there, with coffee and doughnuts, full of ideas about how to get untrained young women into jobs. . . ."

For a moment there was silence . . . and then they started to clap, softly at first, then louder and louder—a proud, triumphal crescendo of sound.

She had talked as an American woman to other American women—and at that moment all the years she had spent at Lyndon's side in the service of their country seemed rich indeed. She had been right when she had said:

"It is a good time to be a woman. It is a good time to be alive!"

Besides, as Lady Bird once pointed out: "The Constitution of the United States outlines the responsibilities and duties of the President. It does not even mention the First Lady. No one—except her husband—chooses her. No one —except her husband and herself—defines her role."

Neither Lady Bird nor her daughters were born or trained for life in high places. They were ordinary American women who overnight became extraordinary. Fame has not turned their heads; they wear its crown with dignity.

Selected Bibliography

*

BOOKS AND ARTICLES

Bell, Jack: *The Johnson Treatment*. Harper & Row, New York, 1965.

First Ladies Hall, The: Smithsonian Publication 4640. Smithsonian Institution, Washington, D.C., 1965.

"First Lady Bird, The": (Cover portrait by Artzybasheff and illustrated story.) *Time* Magazine, August 28, 1964.

Furman, Bess: *White House Profile*. The Bobbs-Merrill Company, Inc., Indianapolis and New York, 1951.

Geyelin, Philip L.: *Lyndon B. Johnson and the World*. Frederick A. Praeger, Inc., New York, 1966.

Hall, Gordon Langley: "The Woman Behind the Man—the Story of Pat Nixon." New York Herald Tribune Syndicate, distributed September 1960.

Hall, Gordon Langley, and Pinchot, Ann: *Jacqueline Kennedy—A Biography*. Frederick Fell, Inc., New York, 1964.

Johnson, Lady Bird: "Lady Bird Johnson Writes Her Own Picture Story." *Life* Magazine, August 13, 1965.

Johnson, Lyndon B.: *My Hope for America*, Random House, New York, 1964.

Johnson, Rebekah Baines: *A Family Album*. With an introduction by President Lyndon Baines Johnson. McGraw-Hill Book Company, New York, 1965.

Leighton, Frances Spatz: "First Lady's First Day." *This Week* Magazine, March 1, 1964.

Means, Marianne: *The Woman in the White House*. Random House, New York, 1963.

Montgomery, Ruth: *Mrs. LBJ*. Holt, Rinehart & Winston, New York, 1964.

"President's Big Sky Country, A": (Photographed by George Silk.) *Life* Magazine, February 14, 1964.

Prindiville, Kathleen: *First Ladies*, 2nd ed. The Macmillan Company, New York, 1964.

Roberts, Charles: *L.B.J.'s Inner Circle.* Delacorte Press, New York, 1965.

Sadler, Christine: "Our Very Busy First Lady." *McCall's* Magazine, March, 1964.

Schreiber, Flora Rheta: "The Personal Story of the First Family." Series of articles in the *Family Weekly*, Montreal, Canada, commencing February 2, 1964.

Report of the Warren Commission on the Assassination of President Kennedy: By the editors of *The New York Times.* McGraw-Hill Book Company, New York, 1964.

The Author

Trained as a journalist, Gordon Langley Hall *has found that his interests, travels and experience have taken him far afield, to the Ojibway Indian reservation of Canada, the Far East, and the American West, and he has made many friends; but when he settles down in his study to write, his only companions are his parrot, Marilyn, and his dogs, Jackie, Richard-Rufus, Annabel-Eliza and Nelly, who always wait for him at home. His list of published books includes his own autobiography, an adult novel, three books for children, and six biographies, including* Princess Margaret *and* Mr. Jefferson's Ladies; *and he is the co-author (with Ann Pinchot) of* Jacqueline Kennedy. *He specializes in writing about America's First Ladies.*

DATE DUE

F	MR 28 '78		
FEB 24 '70			
MAR 17 '70			
FEB 22 '71			
MAR 18 '71			
MAR 30 '71			
APR 5 '73			
APR 30 '73			
MAY 1 '73			
May 10			
FEB 27 '74			
MAY 8 '74			
Ap 16			
FEB 27 '75			
MAR 11 '75			
MAR 20 '75			
MR 6 '78			
GAYLORD			PRINTED IN U.S.A.